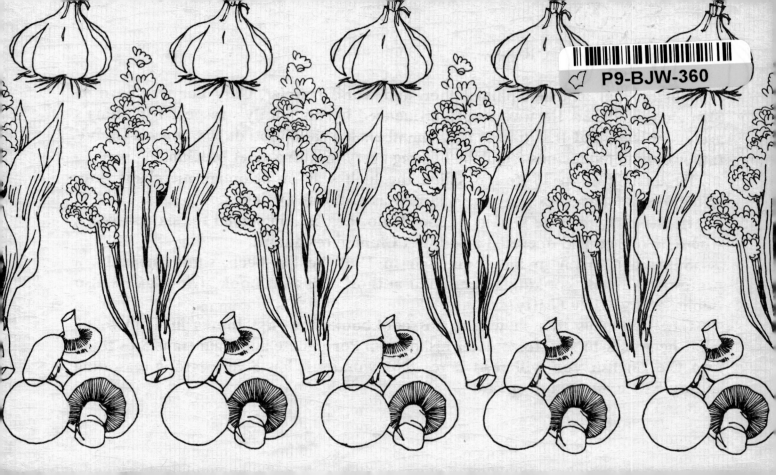

ABOUT THE AUTHOR . . . . .

Master Chef, teacher, philosopher, and world traveler, Gary Lee was born in Shanghai in 1922. He was deeply influenced by his family's respect for China's ageless culture and traditions. He remembers his childhood days when his Grandfather conducted lessons from the I-Ching every morning after breakfast.

He left China in 1946 and sailed the high seas on a foreign merchant ship. After four adventurous years he resigned as Catering Officer.

In the early '50s he settled in Sao Paulo, Brazil, and stayed for sixteen years, where he owned and operated a gourmet Chinese restaurant.

Since his arrival in San Francisco in 1969 he has been, simultaneously, a professional chef, cooking teacher and author. His first book, *The Wok,* is also published by Nitty Gritty.

Gary Lee says that in writing his cookbooks, he first thinks in Chinese of what he wants to say, formulates his ideas in Portuguese and then translates them into the English you will read here. No wonder it has a very strong seasoning of Soy Sauce and many spices!

李一中

GARY LEE
SAN FRANCISCO '72

DEDICATION

Classic Chinese verses are well known for their proven truth. Here is one:

> Plant hopefully a dozen flower bulbs,
>   none of the twelve grows.
> Stick a branch in mud as a marking pole,
>   a shady tree springs up!

Before I became a professional chef I was an unsuccessful Jack-of-all-trades --- Clerk, Lab-man, Amusement Park Manager, Magician, Potato Chip Manufacturer, Photographer, etc., much less had I written a book, even in Chinese.

Maybe I was like the Narcissuses which cannot bloom in the tropics, or the branch from the willow tree which can grow with either end in the mud.

It was lucky that I came to this country where cooking is a hobby and I happened to know a little of the culinary art. I therefore sincerely dedicate this book:

> To my cooking class friends of a hundred-and-one types. I was a bad talker:
>   Thank you for being good listeners.

To Mike without whose drawings this book might have been leafless flowers.

To Peggy -- jobs fun, jobs dull, she always finished with the same willingness.

To Brian, a scrutinizing editor who put half my scrupulous draft into the waste basket, and made this book now readable.

To Earl, the publisher you may talk to without saying, "Sir". But he demands everything to be done to the standard of an Earl! So this book was written.

To Louis and Beth, who corrected the hundreds of errors in my draft, yet insisted that it was not stupidly bad; or I would never dare to write again.

To Hal Hershey, who included me in The Last Whole Earth Catalog, the most delightful honor I ever had from a person unknown to me. So I can only say, "Hey! Hal, Hi!"

To my relatives and grand-daughter Carmem, with an m ? ! .

I am short of words!

Gary Lee
San Francisco, 1972

the chinese VEGETARIAN cook book

by GARY LEE

Illustrated by MIKE NELSON

© Copyright 1972
Nitty Gritty Productions
Concord, California

A Nitty Gritty Book*
Published by
Nitty Gritty Productions
P.O. Box 5457
Concord, California

*Nitty Gritty Books - Trademark
Owned by Nitty Gritty Productions
Concord, California

ISBN 0-911954-20-1

Library of Congress Catalog Card Number: 72-194449

books designed with giving in mind

Pies & Cakes
Yogurt
The Ground Beef Cookbook
Cocktails & Hors d'Oeuvres
Salads & Casseroles
Kid's Party Book
Pressure Cooking
Food Processor Cookbook
Peanuts & Popcorn
Kid's Pets Book
Make It Ahead
   French Cooking
Soups & Stews
Crepes & Omelets

Microwave Cooking
Vegetable Cookbook
Kid's Arts and Crafts
Bread Baking
The Crockery Pot Cookbook
Kid's Garden Book
Classic Greek Cooking
Low Carbohydrate Cookbook
Kid's Cookbook
Italian
Cheese Guide & Cookbook
Miller's German
Quiche & Souffle
To My Daughter, With Love

Natural Foods
Chinese Vegetarian
The Jewish Cookbook
Working Couples
Mexican
Sunday Breakfast
Fisherman's Wharf Cookbook
Charcoal Cookbook
Ice Cream Cookbook
Blender Cookbook
The Wok, a Chinese Cookbook
Japanese Country
Fondue Cookbook

from nitty gritty productions

TABLE OF CONTENTS

HOW TO READ THIS BOOK

I don't expect you to try to read this book from the beginning to the end at one time, although it is carefully edited to hold your interest.

I suggest that you first read the book, but not the recipes, to give you some ideas about Chinese vegetarian cooking. Then pick a simple recipe to try as a starter.

Good luck! To you? No, good luck to me, or you will write me and complain.

WHAT COOKING MEANS IN CHINESE

One big mistake that most readers make is not knowing the difference between cooking and baking. Don't think that you can make anything if you have the right recipe. This may be true in making such things as cakes and breads, but this is not true in cooking even a simple dish such as an omelet.

The baker's basic rules can be clearly defined and can be followed with little difficulty. One can follow such rules as pre-heat the oven to a given number of degrees, sift the flour, melt the butter, measure precisely, and don't examine

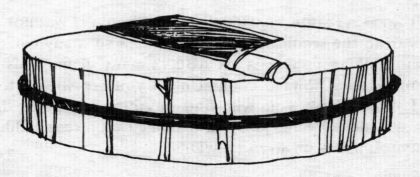

unnecessarily during the baking, etc.

Cooking, especially the Chinese way, is just impossible to define in such a way, as it requires a lot of good sense, judgment, and experience. If you approach cooking as you do baking you will be very disappointed in the results. A good baker can produce hundreds of cakes of a certain kind and nobody can sense any difference. A good cook has no such advantage. In preparing the same dish a hundred times, he is a genius if he can manage eighty percent of them to be of the same quality.

This is the main reason I have written this book. It was not written just to give you recipes from the second page to the last as so many cookbooks do. I do not pretend that cooking is as easy as ABC as many claim. This book is written to help you understand how to cook. Unless you are willing to read and practice carefully, I don't think you will find anything useful in this book—maybe a can-opener will do a better job. I also think that a reasonable amount of effort spent on any job will bring joyful rewards.

THE BEST GROUP OF SECRETS IN COOKING

I notice one interesting characteristic of the art of cooking as compared to the other arts. In painting, for example, you may try as many times as you need to produce a finished piece of art and the length of your life is your time limit. Once you become famous, anything you paint will be kept as a treasure. A modern painter can show you a white piece of paper and call it "Sugar Loves Salt" or call a black piece of paper "Midnight in the Jungle".

A cook is not supposed to cook again and again in order to present you with a satisfactory dish, and he definitely could not give you a dish which you don't like and tell you, "This is a 'Modern Cooking' ".

Once a great sculptor was asked by his students to summarize his artful secrets. The master coldly said, "Just chip away the undesirable part and leave the desirable part!" I agree with him. The secret in cooking is just to buy the right ingredients, cut them accordingly, cook to the right point, and season to taste. Is that all? No, serve them hot, with a good choice of complements, in proper shapes and size of platters, and to the right person.

INGREDIENTS IN CHINESE VEGETARIAN COOKING

Finding the ingredients can be a problem to you so I have tried my best to limit them to those obtainable in most larger American cities.

If you cannot find some of these items in a Chinese market it is possible to buy them mail order from Wing Sing Chong Co., Inc., 931 Clay St., San Francisco, Ca. 94108. If you write to them with an order clearly described, they will advise you of the current price (the same as for their counter customers) and estimated postage cost.

Worrying for those who really have difficulty to get these items, I especially pack this section of the book with home-made methods for some basic ingredients, starting with Gluten.

7

One note about equipment—a 14" Wok is the best for family use, especially for deep frying and making soup (cost $3.50-$5.00) and can make you feel like a real Chinese cook.

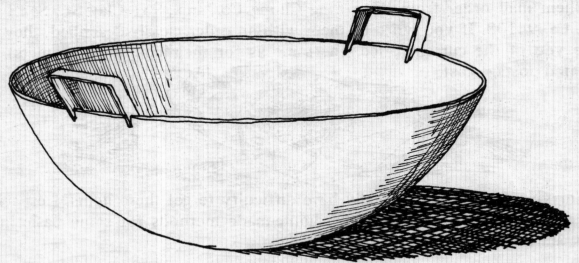

BASICS

Speaking of vegetables in general, most readers and we Chinese, will naturally think of cabbage, lettuce, broccoli, spinach, onions, tomatoes, and so on.

We have tens of other available items in the market, but mostly we limit our cooking to these few choices when vegetables are called for. With these very limited choices, I wonder whether there are really too many interesting combinations or recipes to be discussed.

They say that to make an omelet you need an egg and so . . . to try Chinese vegetarian cooking we certainly need some basic Chinese ingredients which go beyond the vegetables which easily come to mind.

In the section which follows I describe and explain those basic items which I presume you will be interested in making, or in purchasing from your own Chinese markets, or by mail (see page 7 for address of source).

GLUTEN AND HOW TO MAKE IT IN YOUR KITCHEN

Without gluten I wouldn't know how to prepare Chinese vegetarian cooking so that it stands out among other cuisines. So far as I know it is used exclusively by Chinese. The dictionary defines gluten as the viscid, tenacious substance giving adhesiveness to dough, and a nutritious element of food. Making gluten is like making a batch of dough from wheat flour, then washing away the starch, and what you have left is gluten.

Raw gluten is a light greyish color. It looks like rubber and is as sticky as chewed chewing gum. It has no typical taste so it accepts any kind of seasoning to your liking. It can be cooked in water, steamed, or deep-fried. It is soft and can be shaped to any form. It is very delicious when properly used and what a deliciousness, and such a number of variations!

HOME-MADE GLUTEN

Here is the simple procedure to make the dough: Add 1 teaspoon of salt to each cup of water. Add in the water to the wheat flour to make a hard dough. You don't have to care about the amount of water—if it turns too soft just add more flour. That is all there is to it. Shape the dough as a ball. You had better use at least 2 pounds of flour to make it worth your time to do the job.

The best flour is the one for noodle-making because it has more body than all-purpose flour. Keep the ball of dough covered with a wet cloth in the refrigerator overnight.

WASHING THE GLUTEN

I am trying to make it simple for you to follow. If you care to try several times, you definitely will find the best way to meet your own kitchen situation and your personal preference.

Run the tap water gently. Adjust cold in summer and the least warm in winter—this is only thoughtful for your tender fingers, not mine. Hold the dough under the water, pinch, squeeze and rub gently. The movement is as you are washing a kitchen towel. Doing so, the milky starch will be washed away as the running water is falling upon the dough. Do so until there is apparently no more starch coming out. Five minutes is about the time you need for a batch of 2 lbs. of dough.

13

FOR SAVING THE WHEAT-STARCH

You need something to catch the washing water. In order not to be involved with a lot of water, adjust the tap slower and use a big pot to trap the milky washing water. One pot might not be enough. Let the water stand for 5 minutes, which gives you a break, and a rest for the starch to settle. Gently pour off the top part of the water which should be almost clean, and leave the last few inches which contains the starch. Now stir the washing water vigorously and swiftly strain it through a fine cloth. One good method is to use a pair of coarse strainers (big size) with a cloth in between. Support the strainers on the rim of a deep pot or any other functional method.

When starch is settled, bring it to a shallow tray, and dry it in sunshine. Regularly check the dampness and break the lumps before they are completely dry. You may now pass them through a sieve or blend them into powder form. This is wheat-starch.

TO COOK THE RAW GLUTEN

You can cook raw gluten several ways.

Boiling: either in small pieces or whole to be cut up later. Ten minutes.

Steaming: the same as above, it will result in a firmer texture.

Deep-frying: heat the oil at about 330° and drop in marble size pieces of gluten which have been dried with a paper towel. They will swell almost at once to the size of golf balls. Keep pushing them under until they are golden brown.

Storing: cooked and steamed are to be kept in refrigerator as common cooked food. Deep-fried can be kept very long. The Chinese string them as a necklace for a giant, and hang them in a windy cool place out of the sun.

Using: cooked or steamed can be used in many ways, such as in soup, Chinese-frying, stew, or cold-mising. Deep-fried gluten can be used in the same ways except for cold-mixing. Deep-fried gluten can also be used for stuffing, which is a very, very delicious dish.

Remember it is tasteless and spongy; it can be cut or shaped any way you like and it absorbs seasonings easily because of its porous texture. Soy sauce, mushrooms, and sesame oil flavor it nicely.

COOKED (OR STEAMED) GLUTEN WITH GREEN PEPPERS is a representative recipe.

> 1 c gluten, cut into strips
> 1/2 c green pepper, in strips
> 1/2 c bamboo shoots, also in strips
> Deep-fried gluten, four balls per serving
> 1/2 c mung-bean-threads, short length, pre-soaked
> Several pieces of bean curd
> 1 c broth

Simmer them all together till all are tender, about 10 minutes. Season with salt, soy sauce, and sesame oil. When the deep-fried gluten is cooked this way in broth it turns to a soft texture hardly to be described.

MUSHROOMS AND MUNG-BEAN THREADS

Dried black mushrooms and mung-bean threads (sometimes called bean vermi-celli) can usually be purchased in large cities.

Mushrooms can be soaked for as little as 5 minutes in hot water. However, overnight soaking in warm water is better. Clean the dirt out, cut off the stems, if there are any, and squeeze dry before using. The leftover soaking-water should be saved for cooking or broth. Set it aside for a while and then strain it. Throw away the last little batch at the end as it has too many fine sediments. Mushrooms are all-round ingredients which can be used in almost any dish.

Mung-bean threads are soaked in this way: put them in a pot, fill it with hot water, slowly bring to a boil, cover, remove from heat and set aside. After 10 minutes, strain the water out. The leftover soaking-water is useless. The threads are not done yet, but you are going to cook them anyway, and another 5 or 10 minutes will be enough. Don't overcook them or they will be too soft. The mung-bean threads combine well with many other ingredients. Use them with Chinese cabbage. This makes a wonderful, simple, and delicious dish. A small quantity of mushrooms can also be added. Well-cooked and strained threads can be used for cold-mixed dishes. They are tasteless by themselves so they can absorb any seasoning. You can cut them in short lengths and use them for stuffing.

Chinese cabbage, mushrooms, and bamboo shoots can be used with mung-bean threads, either alone, or in a combination of two, or all three together. Pre-soaked mushrooms should be cut to match the shape of Chinese cabbage, that is, sliced or in strips.

MUNG-BEAN SPROUTS

Only mung-bean sprouts are well known to westerners. They are almost taste-less but their crunchiness gives a nice touch to certain dishes. To use mung-bean sprouts for cold-mixing, or fresh tossed salad, you merely drain them. The typical Chinese way is to dump the fresh sprouts into hot water, say 160°, for 10 seconds. Drain them and rinse with cold tap water and drain again. The dumping in hot water gets rid of the raw taste and the cold water rinse stops the heat which would turn them soggy. Never parboil mung-bean sprouts. If they are used for a cooked dish, they should be added just before serving. They should never be cooked over 10 seconds while blending with the already cooked food with season-ing and salt.

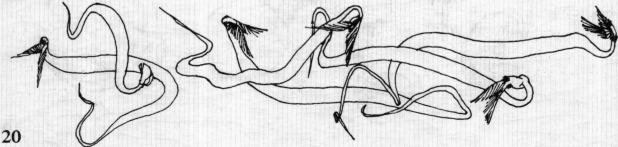

HOW TO MAKE SOY BEAN MILK

I sincerely hope this will help you to sprout your interest and give you fun in Chinese vegetarian cooking. I choose the soy bean milk as a first step for you. This will also serve as a test for your degree of fondness of cooking. If you think this is too tedious and not the way you like to cook, the rest of this book will probably help you very little.

Buy the best quality of soy beans. Now I will tell you the steps in preparing the beans. If your beans came from a farmer without a good machine for packing they might have sand or small stones mixed in with them. Washing is the only way to get rid of the dirt. A simple washing under cold tap water with a colander will do this job. After washing, place the beans in a container. Fill it with cold water in the summer and warm water of 68° in the winter.

We are not going to industrialize our milk making. Therefore, we just follow the simple and practical ways. Normally overnight soaking is enough but the actual surrounding temperature makes the difference. The cooler the temperature the longer the time that will be needed. However, by the next day you pick out

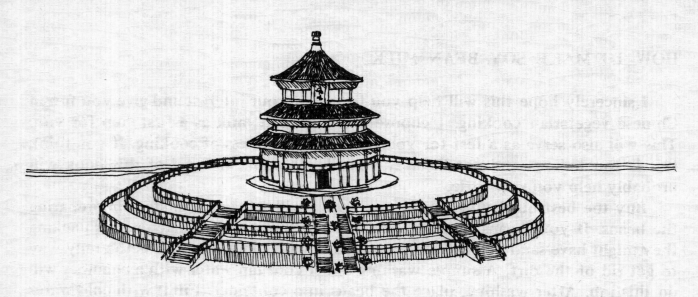

one of the beans and break it apart with your thumb and first finger. When the bean is separated into two halves, see if the central part shows a tiny dent. (Normally they are smooth.) If the dent has appeared the beans are well soaked and it is time to start making the milk. This point is very important as starting too soon or waiting too late will lessen the production of milk.

For making the milk, fill your blender with the soaked beans and water. The beans should not be over one-third the capacity or it will be too difficult for the blender. You don't have to blend them too long. As soon as the water turns milky and the beans are broken down to sand-size particles you have blended them enough. Normal high speed is enough and don't over-blend them. After the blending, filter through a cheesecloth. Boil the milky solution for 5 minutes. It is then ready to serve.

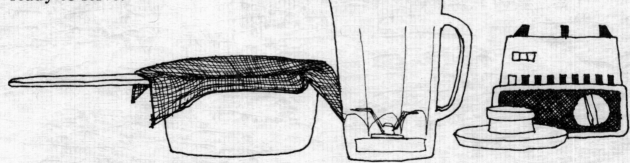

TO SERVE THE BEAN-MILK

Bean-milk has a strong soy flavor. It can be served either hot or cold—it is milk. The flavor is a delight to some but disagreeable to others—especially young children. The easiest way to overcome the strong flavor is to serve it with a little bit of other flavor added—such as chocolate—and sweeten with sugar to taste. In northern China, bean-milk is served as a delicious main course for breakfast seasoned with soy sauce and sesame oil. You may add chopped green onions for more color and flavor. The most tasteful way is to add a little pinch of the famous Sze-chwan preserved vegetables. They should be very finely chopped. Some people like to add a few drops of hot chili oil. If you do this, I do not recommend serving it to children. Remember, don't use only the soy sauce to season the bean milk. Allow a small amount of salt plus soy sauce. If you don't have sesame oil, you should use a few drops of cooking oil.

WHAT TO DO WITH THE RESIDUE?

Almost everything created by nature can be used. At present too much is wasted. Here is an interesting way to use the residue from the bean-milk. It actually is a very useful food source.

Heat the bean residue in a wok or a non-sticking pan and add "left-over sauce" to it. Left-over sauce is from whatever kind of a cooked dish you have had and are generally wasted away into the sink. Do you not do this? But you can keep them, no matter how little or how much, for this recipe for residue of bean. In vegetarian cooking almost any sauce will be good here. Keep adding left-over sauces until one day the residue tastes salty enough and the oil in the sauces has made the residue smooth and tasty. You serve it as you do mashed potatoes.

As I wrote in my book, *The Wok*, "You will be surprised that Chinese cooking in some ways is really much simpler than you would imagine and you can apply these Chinese cooking techniques to your own cooking. It can improve your cooking style no matter how original it may be."

HOW TO GROW SOY BEAN SPROUTS

Soak soy beans in water, enough to cover plus 2 more inches. Overnight is usually enough.

Drain the soaking water. DON'T throw it away! It is very tasteful for making soup or to use as a broth. It bears a strong bean flavor and should be boiled for a while to let the taste smooth out.

Keep the well-soaked beans in a colander and cover with a folded kitchen towel. The colander should be kept out of the sunshine. That is why in the Shanghai dialect, when we refer to someone who has suddenly disappeared from the society he frequented, we say, "he is sprouting at his home."

You are not going to install a machine to water the beans so you can just water them early in the morning, during the meal hours, and the last thing before you go to bed. The number of times that you water per day is very flexible. Pour cold water through the covering towel two or three times in each watering. Then just leave it on the sink to drain by itself. No one can resist the desire to examine the stage of sprouting during the required several days. It is interesting to see them grow longer and longer roots. Now, here is another thing we can learn from sprouting and apply it to the science of human behavior. If some weight is placed on top of the towel it presses the sprouting beans. The sprouts try to resist the weight and fight to grow upwards. The weight will help the beans to sprout more as compared to another batch without the pressing weight. Of course, everything has a limit and if you put too much weight on the beans you will certainly kill the sprouting.

Preparing bean sprouts is much like dealing with the younger generation. I must decide whether or not to use no weight, some weight, or a lot of weight? This also applies in dealing with our bad habits or our enemies.

As I said before, the sprouting will take several days. The dictionary says several means more than two but not many. In Chinese we define several as "it must be three, or it is not several." However, you should not care about the exact number of days needed. Examine the sprouts during the watering. They should reach a length of about two inches and always stay a shining white color. If they turn a slight reddish-brown they are over-mature. In that case they should be used right away. Otherwise, you may use part of them for cooking and keep the rest for one more day. Recipes for using sprouts will be found elsewhere in this book.

TRIMMING THE SPROUTS

This is a time consuming job. That is why, in the United States, where labor is very costful, most restaurants serve sprouts without trimming them. For mung-bean sprouts the thin roots should be trimmed away. You can do this with your fingernails. That is why I ask my wife to do it. I have good reason as my nails are shorter and do not work as well as hers.

In serving mung-bean sprouts as a very delicate dish, the heads of sprouts are also trimmed away. Chinese menus refer to this dish as "silver-sprouts". For soy bean sprouts you leave the heads but trim the roots as the tiny roots are tasteless and spoil the crunchiness of the sprouts. Both kinds of beans have hulls. This hull is not at all tasty and should be separated during the watering and final washing. The hull is nature's way of protecting the beans by sealing each one individually. They come loose during the sprouting. Wash the sprouted beans in a deeply filled sink. The loose hulls are generally floating on top so it will not be too difficult to separate them.

BRINED VEGETABLES

Brined vegetables are typical Sze-chwan products. You can hardly match a hot-dish (seasoning) to those of Sze-chwan chefs because all vegetables used in their hot-dishes have been treated in brine and have very exquisite taste.

Brined vegetables are excellent to be served cold, as complementary dishes or as ingredients in hot-dishes. For a cold or complementary dish you take them from the brining jar and serve them just as they are. They're something like pickles but they are milder. Making brined vegetables is a handy way to have something always ready to serve.

The procedure for making them is simple. It is not necessary to have a specially designed jar—you can use an unglazed earthenware jar or a wide-mouth glass jar. Loosely cover the jar and keep it in a cool place. In hot weather you should put the jar in the refrigerator.

TO PREPARE THE BRINE you need the following ingredients: Salt—rock salt is preferred—use plenty to make the water very salty; Water—boil it awhile, then add the salt and let it cool; Flower pepper—use coriander seeds if flower pepper is not available—use five seeds per cup of water; Hot chili pepper—use one fresh red chili pepper per ten cups of water—you may also use dried chili powder.

VEGETABLES SUITABLE FOR BRINE

Green leafy vegetables should not be used.

Chinese cabbage (also called Napa cabbage)—Use the white part only. This is the best cabbage to use.

Cabbage—This is second choice. Cut in small pieces—no bits.

Carrots—These are good but not very exciting.

Bell Peppers—These are suitable only for use in hot-seasoning cooking. Don't over-brine them.

Turnips and Radishes—These give a good refreshing sharp taste.

Cauliflower and Cucumber—These are both good. The cauliflower needs to stay in the brine longer than the cucumber.

PREPARING THE VEGETABLES TO BE BRINED

In general all vegetables should be well cleaned, drained, or wiped with a paper towel. Cabbage should be cut in pieces about the size of a domino or larger. Carrots should be cut in thin slices, about one-eighth of an inch thick. It is best to cut small carrots diagonally. Bell peppers should be cut in pieces after removing veins and seeds. Turnips should be cut in pieces according to their shape. Small radishes can be mashed with a plank or the side of a cleaver but don't mash them too much. The purpose is only to split them somehow so the brine can easily penetrate the radish. You use only the flower part of the cauliflower leaving on one-half inch of the stem. Cucumbers should not be peeled but the seeds should be removed. Cut them into thick slices or sticks.

TIME NEEDED FOR BRINING THE VEGETABLES

The time needed for brining the vegetables will depend on the texture of the various vegetables and the room temperature. The cooler the temperature the longer the time needed. The best way to tell if the vegetables are ready is to try a tiny bite. If they are underdeveloped leave them a few more days. With experience you will be able to tell by their appearance.

Once in a while add a teaspoon of a strong-tasting Chinese wine. If you are unable to obtain it, vodka may be used. The purpose of the alcohol is to prevent mold from forming. Always use clean tools to bring the vegetables from the jar. Never allow any oil to touch the brine.

As vegetables will absorb the salt from the brine, as each new batch is added, salt should also be added. It is impossible to add the salt by exact measurements. Instead you can judge the amount of salt needed by tasting the brine or the brined vegetables.

HOW TO SERVE THE BRINED VEGETABLES

Congee is served at a traditional Chinese breakfast. Brined vegetables can be served with congee as a variation. For the other meals you can serve them as a side dish, somewhat like a fresh tossed salad. You can serve them as they are or add a few drops of oil. In cooking any hot-seasoned dish you can add brined vegetables to give a different flavor. Just pick them out, drain them, and cut them to the right shape depending on the other ingredients in the dish.

THE LENGTH OF THE TIME TO KEEP THE BRINE

Your brine jar can last indefinitely if you are careful to let no impurities enter the brine. In China it is not unusual for a brine jar to last fifty years. In theory the older your brine the stronger it is. The brine jar should be kept in a cool and dark place.

SALTED VEGETABLES

The Chinese have still another way with vegetables and this has to do with turnip leaves, chard and mustard greens.

I don't know how to produce a giant from a jar but I can almost bring the giant into the jar. Consider a big bunch of these vegetables as the giant and a small bottle as a jar. I wash them carefully and then cut into tiny strips. If you use a common kitchen tray, you need no more than 2 teaspoons of salt for the whole trayful of vegetables piled an inch high. Sprinkle them with salt, mixing evenly. Wait a little while and then rub them between your hands to work the salt into them. The natural juices will begin to come out, they begin to turn soft, and you can begin to force them into a small bottle. Use your thumb to force them down neatly around all the edges. By pressing and forcing, the juice will come out and the volume will decrease unbelievably. This is why I say you can bring the giant into the jar.

Save the excess juice for soup and tightly cover the well packed vegetables. Leave the jar outside the refrigerator but in a cool place for a day or two. Then refrigerate for three or four days more. Cook with oil and add complements such as bamboo shoots, bean curd, etc.

Some people like these vegetables salty and sour. To achieve the two flavors rinse the vegetables with rice washing-water. The little starch will turn sour after several days. The salting process is the same. Very appetizing.

SOURED (OR SALTED) VEGETABLES WITH BEAN CURD SOUP

1 c vegetables, loosened from the jar
1 c bean curd strips
3 T oil

Some soy sauce
1 t sugar

Heat the oil and cook the vegetables for 10 seconds; add enough water to make a soup. Season. Bring to a boil, simmer for 2 minutes, and serve. Garnish with sesame oil.

BROTH FOR CHINESE VEGETARIAN COOKING

Broth is the base of successful cooking in this field of cuisine. So far I have found only one ready-made "seasoning and broth" which the manufacturer claimed was both meat-free and fat-free. Thanks to the regulation of food packaging the manufacturer is obliged to state the contents in the order of ingredients used the most: "MSG, salt, onion and celery, coloring and spice."

Broth should be both colorless and versatile to meet every possible demand. I have always said that the Chinese have a tradition of doing things as simply as possible. Chinese cooking is the simplest of all the cuisines I have studied. In our broth for vegetarian cooking we use only soy bean sprouts. Please note that only soy bean sprouts are used, not sprouts made from mung beans. The soy bean has been given a very flattering name by someone in the West who called it "The Wonderful Bean," and without it Chinese vegetarian cooking would be little different from other types of cooking.

I think it is very reasonable of me to ask you to get some soy beans. They can be kept for a very long time. The beans themselves can be used for making broth but the taste is too strong and obvious. When you turn the soy beans into sprouts, which can be used in many ways in Chinese cooking, you have the right ingredient for making a delicious and delicate broth. It is very clear and almost colorless and it blends very well with almost all kinds of vegetables.

In making broth there is no standard proportion of sprouts to water. You can use one cup of sprouts to four to six cups of water. Bring them to a boil and then simmer for an hour. You need a weaker broth for soup and a stronger one for cooking. The more water you add the weaker the broth, and vice versa. Simple as that. Your personal taste will also be your guide and after a few times you'll have no difficulty and you'll not need to measure sprouts and water at all.

Broth can be seasoned with salt or soy sauce. Use plain preheated cooking oil in salt-seasoned broth for smoothness. Use sesame oil in broth seasoned with soy sauce for flavor. In both cases just a few drops of oil should be used. If you like, add some pepper.

PRE-HEATED OIL IN VEGETARIAN COOKING

In classic Chinese vegetarian cooking chefs use only pre-heated oil. You heat a bottle of oil to about 300 degrees. Add in, to your personal taste, one small slice of ginger root and/or several stalks of green onions. Turn off the heat and let the ginger, or onion, or both, bubble until the moisture is out. The flavor is now in the oil. Cool it and bottle for further use in cooking. Only the family of garlic ginger root, green onions, leeks, and the like are used to season pre-heated oil.

MIXED VEGETABLE DRESSING

All four members of my family -- my daughters, Vida and Linda, my wife, Hedy -- are fond of cooking but in different ways. I like everything about cooking. Since they all make frank and almost merciless verdicts about my cooking, I worked out this dressing to please them. I originally prepared it as a sauce to serve with barbecue, but we had too much left over so I used it to dress fresh lettuce the next day. It is very good, indeed.

Dice a firm tomato into pea-size squares. This should fill about a cup. Dice one onion and one-fourth of a bell pepper into pea-size pieces, salt them, and set aside for ten minutes. The salt will bring out the flavor of the onions and peppers. To satisfy my family food-jury, I have to rinse the onions and peppers with boiling water from a kettle. I then rinse with cold tap water so they don't become soggy. Now the onions and bell peppers are rid of the raw taste my family dislikes. Chop some fresh coriander coarsely. This is the most important ingredient so parsley will do only if you can't find fresh coriander.

When the rinsed onions and peppers are well drained, mix them with the pieces of tomato. Add enough vinegar to barely cover the whole batch in a deep wide-mouth jar. Add 2 teaspoons of salt and 2 teaspoons of sugar. Add one-fourth cup of peanut oil and the chopped coriander. Shake the jar well. You may serve it now but my family prefers it smoother. Blend it about three seconds in a blender or mash the tomato and chop the rest more finely.

SAUCES FOR VEGETABLES

CREAM SAUCE, which by name sounds as the same as in non-Chinese cooking, but is completely different in preparation and takes only 2 minutes. Bring the desired amount of broth to a boil, season with salt and mix cornstarch with milk to thicken. Add more oil to make it smoother, add a pinch of pepper, and pour over the prepared vegetables. Use the cream sauce over Chinese cabbage or cauliflower. Prepare both this way: simmer until done, season only with salt, drain well, and place them neatly on a platter. Drain the vegetables again by tilting the platter while the sauce is being prepared.

SOY-SAUCE SAUCE—I have to use the word, "sauce," twice to distinguish it as a thickened sauce made from soy-sauce—bring the broth to a boil, season with soy-sauce, sugar, and thicken with cornstarch. Add oil and also some sesame oil before serving. This has many uses with pre-cooked vegetables of many kinds, bean curd, etc.

46

GINGER SAUCE (one cup)

Clove of garlic, mashed
3 slices ginger root—size of a quarter
Stalk of celery—peel off the tough outer layer
  and use the leaves
1/2 a bell pepper
1/2 a firm tomato
1 small onion

2 T ketchup
2 T soy-sauce
1 t sugar
1 c water or broth
1 t sesame oil
1 T cornstarch mixed
  with 3 T water

Put 3 tablespoons of oil in a wok. When the oil is hot, add in the garlic and ginger and cook for 5 seconds to bring out their flavors. Add the rest of the ingredients and cook for five minutes at the boiling state. Thicken with cornstarch and serve.

COLD-MIXING SAUCE

This is really very simple. Use the following proportions:

> 1 T soy sauce
> 1 t sesame oil
> 1/3 t sugar (only for harmonizing the taste)

You may also add in 1 T of vinegar. If you do, use one more T of sugar. If you like hot seasoning you may add chili powder, paste, or sauce.

THICKENING

Except for deep-fried dishes served by themselves, most dishes have a sauce which should be thickened so it will cling to the food. This makes the food taste better. However if you thicken the sauce too much you end up with baby food.

In Chinese cooking only corn starch is used for thickening while Westerners use flour. Our sauces are light and shining while those thickened with flour are heavy and dull. In general practice the amount of starch to use can never be put in measurements. The only guide I can give you is to mix the starch with cold water, about one part of starch to two or three parts of water. Add in this mixture to the sauce, little by little, until the desired density is reached. In adding the water-mixed starch, it must be well stirred just before adding unless you like to serve sauce in numbers of lumps instead of spoonfuls. Remember, it takes a few more seconds of cooking to thicken the mixture. If it seems too thin it may be just right after another five seconds of cooking.

During the thickening the sauce would always be boiling and it should be stirred constantly. It is the oil that makes the sauce smooth. If you have a large amount of sauce to thicken you may have to add more oil. The additional oil can be added at any time—before, during, or after the cooking.

COLD MIXED VEGETABLES (Chinese tossed green salad)

I will now define salting and squeezing in detail. Most vegetables (cabbage, Chinese cabbage, cucumber) used in cold-mixing are salted and squeezed. To salt you sprinkle lightly with salt. Don't worry about measuring the salt. Just spread the whole batch of vegetables rather flat and lightly sprinkle with salt from a shaker. The salt is used as an astringent to take out the excess moisture. It should not be done in a hurry. Toss the vegetables thoroughly and leave them in the refrigerator at least thirty minutes. If you are rushed for time you may toss them and squeeze them at the same time for five minutes. Of course this is not the most desirable method. The purpose of squeezing is to squeeze out the natural moisture. Use both hands. Give the vegetables a firm pressing, press out the moisture.

I like the natural juices of many vegetables so I save the juices to cook in soup. This reminds me of a story of a monkey trainer: Once there was a monkey trainer who used to give 3 peaches to each of his monkeys in the morning, and 4 in the afternoon. One day his assistant gave 4 in the morning and 3 in the afternoon. But, the monkeys complained for one peach was short in their daily ration! Please don't think I am always writing things which seem to have nothing to do with cooking. I am cautious. I don't like to receive a letter from a reader who might be a nutritionist, telling me vitamins were wasted. It is just as simple as 4 plus 3, or 3 plus 4. Your vitamins are now in the soup.

Salting and squeezing many vegetables makes them firmer and helps them retain crispness without a raw taste which is not appreciated by Chinese. In unsalted and unsqueezed vegetables the natural moisture already occupies all the space in their texture, leaving no room for seasoning to get in. It is like the biggest event in 1971 when the United Nations ousted the Nationalist Chinese because two can't share one seat. In cooking we substitute the original and natural juices with tasteful seasoning, and I hope it will be the same with the United Nations.

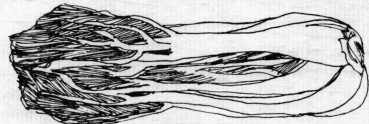

QUENCHING EGG PLANT OR GREEN PEPPER

Take small pieces of green pepper or egg plant that have been deep-fried until done and are very hot. Dump them immediately into a seasoned mixture. I call this technique "quenching." The sudden change of temperature will change the texture of the food and let the seasoning get inside of it. In vegetarian cooking, I find that only eggplants and bell peppers are good for the quenching technique. Prepare your quenching solution first so it will be available as soon as you take the vegetables from the oil.

QUENCHING SOLUTION

1/2 cup of soy sauce
1/2 cup of water
1/6 cup of sugar or to taste
Crushed garlic or garlic salt—for eggplant, only

TO BURN WITH OIL

This is a simple cooking term. Heat the oil very hot, almost smoking, and pour it on the dish calling for "burn it with heated oil". The hot oil is used to bring out the aroma of herbs such as green onions, coriander, ginger root, and the like.

EGG SKINS AND EGG STRIPS (Chinese crepes)

A very simple and useful way to make a dish much more delightful in taste and appearance is to use egg skins or egg strips. Beat the eggs well but don't overdo it. The best way I have found is to add a very small amount of salt during the beating and strain the eggs through a tea-strainer afterward. This gives a much smoother mixture and helps to make the egg skin, or crepe as you may call it, very thin and smooth. This method also gives more egg skins per egg as compared to the unstrained egg mixture.

To make the egg skin, which should be round if you wish to use it to wrap stuffing, use a wok or skillet. If you plan to cut the egg skin into egg strips you may use less care in forming its shape. The cookware should be hot, but not extremely so. Once the cookware comes to the right temperature the next one will always need one lower setting of heat. However, during the making, if the cookware is too hot, just lift it away from the heat. The egg skin should be cooked slowly and evenly. Use only a few drops of oil which you should rub in with a paper dab. Pay close attention to the egg skin edges and give them more heat until they loosen from the cookware.

If a seldom used, or slightly burned wok is used, the edges will sometimes stick on the wok. Add a few drops of oil on the problem areas of the edge as this will help to loosen them so you can turn them over. The first side will take about thirty seconds to form and the second side will only need about five seconds as the egg skin is almost cooked. It is a very simple matter to add drops of oil even if you don't have an oil dispenser. A very ancient design that meets all modern requirements is the chopstick. Use one chopstick to catch oil from a bottle and drip the drops of oil where you need them. Simple?

Normally one egg can be made into two pieces of eight-inch skin. However this will depend upon the thickness you make them. After you have finished the job you have a skin that can be used as a wrapping for stuffing or can be cut into strips.

First cut the egg skin into strips about one inch wide. Stack them and cut again into narrow strips of say one-eighth to one-fourth inch, depending on the

demand. **For garnishing, say for soup, you need them very narrow. For complements in a dish, such as a cold-mixed dish, you need them wider.**

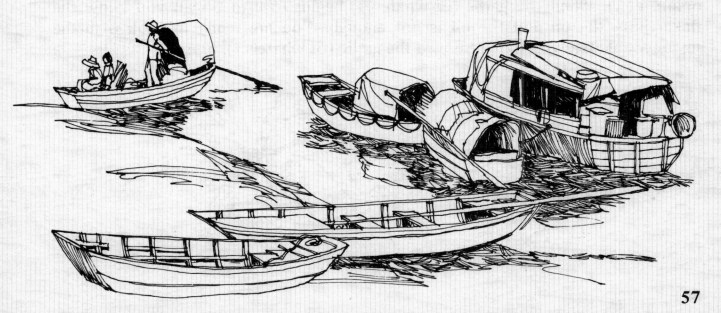

COOKING WITH GARLIC (or whatever) SEASONED OIL

   Here is a simple method: turn the heat to the highest, place a dry pan over the heat and add the amount of oil called for in the recipe. Then add garlic (or ginger, onion, etc.). When the garlic (or whatever) begins to turn brown you know the flavor is in the oil and the oil is hot enough. You are ready to cook with the seasoned oil after you have removed the garlic (or whatever). Simple?

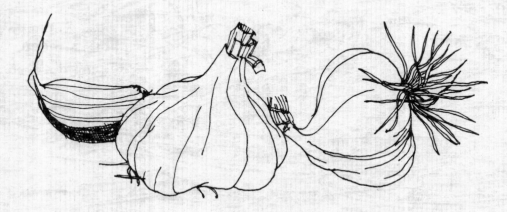

DEEP-FRIED VEGETABLES

Some vegetables lend themselves nicely to this method of cooking:

Eggplant--Use raw slices seasoned with salt and pepper.

Cauliflower--Boil for short time, drain, rinse until cold, drain thoroughly. Salt and pepper.

Carrots--Boil until almost done. Cool. Cut in slices or short sticks. Salt and pepper.

Green pepper--Cut into pieces and cook for short time in oil seasoned with salt.

To fry, dump the prepared vegetables into any one of several kinds of Chinese

batters. You can use a soft one made of flour, baking powder and water or, if you like a crispy batter, here is an excellent one:

> 3 parts self-rising flour
> 1 part cornstarch
> 2 parts water
> 1/10 part peanut oil

Sift the flour and cornstarch into a deep mixing bowl. Add the peanut oil by pouring into the edge of the flour and cornstarch mix. Gradually add in the water, little by little, stirring slowly and gently with a spoon. You can check the density of the batter by lifting a spoonful and letting it drop back into the bowl. It should run slowly and smoothly and it is just right.

Put only a few pieces of the prepared vegetables into the batter at one time or you will get them messy. Pick them out with chopsticks or spoon, (chopsticks are better), let the excess batter fall off and carry them gently to the oil, preheated to 340°. Don't disturb them in the first 5 seconds, then gently turn them around and over until the batter is lightly golden brown.

All of these vegetables can also be double-fried. You can deep-fry them hours before serving time or even the night before. Keep them in a cold place, and when it is time to serve them just deep-fry again for a few seconds. This is how restaurants manage to fill orders rapidly. The result is even better than single frying. Serve with soy sauce or seasoned salt.

SUMMARY ABOUT BASIC SEASONING IN VEGETARIAN COOKING

Salt is nicknamed Super-taste in some regions. It is real, indeed. When a dish is correctly salted you have done half the job. In general, a pinch of salt in the oil before adding any vegetables will increase the temperature of the oil and will draw out the natural moisture in the vegetables. It will also prevent burning of drier vegetables. Most Chinese housewives do this but don't know why. Their mothers did not explain it to them because their grandmothers did not know either.

If you like vegetables crispy, rather than soft and soggy, add the salt later, just before serving.

Never add salt to any kind of beans during simmering because it hardens the protein and they take longer to cook. On the other hand, when you want to brown bean curd it will go faster and easier if you do soak the curd in salted water for awhile.

In Chinese cooking, sugar is used not so much to sweeten but rather to harmonize a tasty saltiness. In my kitchen I use sugar from a salt shaker with 30 small holes in a 1-1/2 inch diameter top. With one shake I manage the little amount of sugar for a standard portion of food.

As I'm sure you already know, soy sauce is the characteristic Chinese seasoning. You can buy specially flavored soy sauces—mushroom flavored, shrimp seasoned, etc., but don't. The manufacturers are only trying to spray a rose with perfume. I use only regular soy sauce. Different brands have different amounts of salt added so you may want to try several to find your own desired amount of saltiness and then stick with that.

In the U.S. we have little choice but peanut oil. Most other vegetable oils contain a blend of cottonseed oil which has a strong smell and is greasy for cooking. Corn oil cannot stand the high temperatures we use in Chinese cooking and we never use olive oil. Soy bean oil is commonly used in China and is a semi-dry oil which is very good for deep-frying but is generally unobtainable here.

Sesame oil is for garnishing. If you cannot find it in your stores you can make your own easily, for a little will go a long way in garnishing. Brown a cup of sesame seeds in a dry skillet or toast them in the oven. Try medium heat for browning or 300° in the oven. When you catch the smell of lightly burning it is time to stop. Put the seeds and one cup of oil in the blender and run at high speed for one minute. Strain, and the oil will bear the aroma of sesame. The strength of the aroma and taste will depend upon the degree of toasting—the longer the toasting the stronger the flavor. Not only are you able to satisfy your own taste but you now have a by-product of sesame paste which you can use in cold mixing—or try as peanut butter.

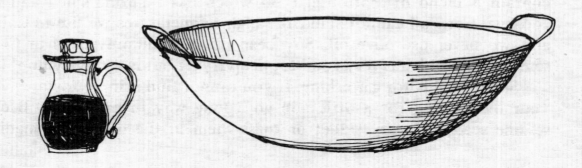

TO GO WITH WHAT?

At first I did not know what my cooking class students meant when they asked me, "What is this dish to go with?" Then they patiently explained to me, for instance, steak goes with baked potatoes, hamburger with French-fries, and poached fish goes with mashed potatoes. I think I am going to plant potatoes.

After long study and comparing, here is my answer: everything goes with rice (but we don't count that). Chinese menus are contrary to the Marriage Computer—we match our dishes by dismatching. Light seasoned dish goes with heavy one. Delicate dish followed by stronger. One dish with a lot of sauce, the other dry. I think this is not too difficult for you to understand our Chinese way in menus.

INDEXING OF RECIPES

Because this is not conventional cooking it is not practical to arrange them in groups as Soups, Entrees, Desserts, etc.

I like also to share my cooking practice with readers. Except for a rather formal dinner, or occasionally I suddenly want a particular dish, my daily cooking routine is to see what I have on hand, then study what to do with them, avoiding what was done the day before. When I am shopping I give the first choice to vegetables and fruits in season and keep them reasonably in stock. Leftovers are always to be consumed in the following meal. When the amount is too much, I carefully keep them for several days later.

For easy reference, I group selected recipes under one item and in alphabetical order.

The Apple dessert (page 70) is very classic and is described in full detail, while under the Banana (page 79) you are asked to refer to the Apple, only the Banana may be prepared with stuffing so you are asked to refer to Sweet-stuffing (page 88). If you go through the whole book first by heading (don't read the recipes) you will know roughly how many references there are in this book.

APPLE

This is a very classic Mandarin dish, although it is now served by all kinds of Chinese restaurants around the world. Each has its own name—Crystal Apple, Carameled Apple, Apple with Sugar Threads, etc.

Buy firm and crisp apples if you can. Peel, cut into eighths and trim out the core. Trim off the sharp points. Dust them with flour before you dip them in the batter for deep-frying. See Batter for deep-frying. Dip them in the batter, cover completely and then gently drop into oil heated in a wok at around 330°. With a clean spoon baste hot oil over top of the apple piece for about 5 seconds, then turn it over in the oil and don't disturb for another 5 seconds.

Fry them one at a time but at 10 seconds each it should take you hardly any time at all.

One small apple should serve two. You may serve them golden brown, or you may add caramel sugar. Serve the very hot apples in a bowl and provide each guest with a small bowl of ice cold water. The hot apple pieces are dipped in the water and then eaten.

ARROWROOT

In conventional cooking, Chinese use arrowroot to absorb excess meat fat—the same role as using potatoes in a meat stew. In vegetarian cooking we have to use a good amount of peanut oil to make it smoother.

STEWED ARROWROOT

3 T peanut oil
8 oz arrowroot peeled, rolling cut
1 clove garlic, crushed
1/2 t salt
1 T sugar
2 T soy sauce

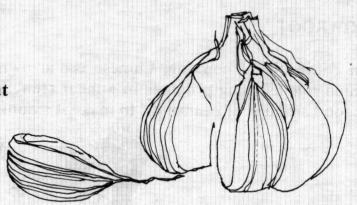

Heat a small pot with oil, add in the garlic (see page 58, Cooking with garlic seasoned oil), brown the arrowroot for 30 seconds, now use rather medium heat; add in seasonings, give them 5 seconds more cooking; add in water, bring to a boil, then simmer for 20 minutes or until done. Arrowroot is served traditionally during the "Full-moon Festival" as a snack or a dessert.

Another method is to cook unpeeled arrowroot in water until done. Drain and let cool for easy handling. Serve on a small saucer with sugar at one side. Each person peels his own and dips the desired amount of sugar to his taste.

ASPARAGUS

Consider I was Chinese-born and a very average Chinese. I presume many of my fellow countrymen only know asparagus in cans. Fresh asparagus has such a deliciousness and a pleasant color if you don't overcook them. Chinese never miss any item which they can use in their cooking, so during the season of asparagus you find it is always used in every Chinese restaurant. I don't know who first found out that it blends well with black-beans (fermented). Notice this in Chinese restaurants and check its truthfulness. By adding black-bean paste I feel it is very fair to accept them in this Chinese vegetarian cookbook.

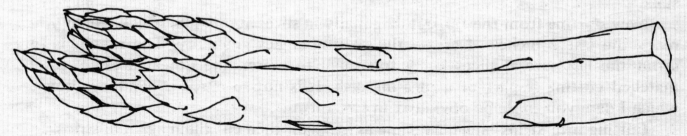

Don't let the shape fool you. You can decide the tenderness by pinching with your fingers at the larger end. The very last half inch is usually too tough for cooking. I like to cook every dish neatly. So I use a potato peeler to peel very gently the outer and rather tough layer. I even trim the tender tips very lightly to have them in firmer and smoother state, because these tiny tender buds will turn a dish messy. I lose in volume, but I gain in appearance, which is the price we have to pay for caring. Cut the roots up to the part where you feel they are tender enough—generally it ranges from 1/4" to an inch, depending on the quality of the stalk.

Now starting from the tip, cut diagonally in slices about 1/8" thick. When you reach the last 2 inches, decrease the cutting angles gradually. The reason is to avoid the last several slices being too small to match the other slices. A good matched cutting is part of a pleasing dish. It is not so much as your eyebrows, which I dare you to shape obviously in two forms.

Cutting into strips—start the same as in slices, then cut them again in strips. In this case the first cut should be somewhat thicker than an ordinary slice.

To cook—forget all other suggested timing in cooking asparagus. Heat the oil, season it with garlic and mashed black-bean (fermented). Add the asparagus and Chinese-fry, adding water by the spoonful, just enough to create steam to cook the asparagus. Keep on high heat and add water only if necessary. For a small batch, 5 minutes will be more than enough.

Seasoning guide for 1 pound of trimmed asparagus
2 t mashed black-beans
1 clove garlic, crushed
1 T soy sauce
2 t sugar
1 t sesame oil before serving

Variations: Asparagus with onion cut in slices, proportion 1 : 1. The same, plus

Black Fugus. Very little amount of fugus will be needed, as the fugus is a complement.

Chinese appreciate canned asparagus. For a banquet it is served drained as part of an assorted cold-dish. For a hot dish heat the asparagus in broth, drain, lay them on a platter. Use the juice from the can, thicken it with milk, cornstarch and oil. As milk and cornstarch are added in, add more salt to taste. Pour the sauce over the asparagus and serve.

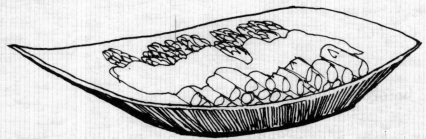

AVOCADO

Chinese call it Fruit-of-butter and it is very expensive in Hong Kong. One of our friends, who detests it, calls the avocado Fruit-of-soap.

The only method which I know that Chinese use is to chill the avocado (whole) for several hours; beat sugar into about 1/2 to 1/4 cup of heavy cream; add 1/4 t salt. They then cut the avocado in halves, scoop out the pulp and roughly cut with a fork, adding 1 t of fresh lemon juice, and top with the sweetened cream.

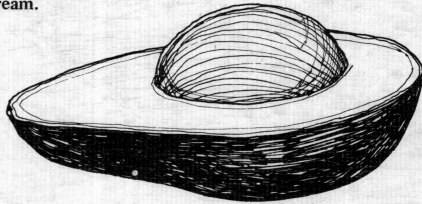

BANANA

You prepare these exactly the same way as apples for deep-frying. Buy firm fruit, peel and cut the points, then cut in chunks the same length as the diameter. For this dish you can use a garnish of 1 c of confectioners' sugar and 1 T of cinnamon powder. Simply roll the deep-fried banana in it and serve.

BANANA WITH STUFFING

Cut the tips, then cut lengthwise in halves. Using a small spoon, scoop out some of the center to give space for stuffing. Don't overdo it or you will break the banana. Fill one of the halves, slightly heaping, with Sweet Stuffing and close with the other half, firmly. Cut in chunks, dust the cut ends with cornstarch and proceed with deep-frying as with simple apple and banana.

BARLEY

This is used in stuffing for conventional cooking but in vegetarian cooking it is used as a soup or a kind of Chinese dessert. 1 c of barley, 3 quarts of water and sugar to taste. Soak the barley overnight, bring it to a boil for 5 minutes, thicken with cornstarch and serve. Use rock sugar if available. This can also be served cold in summer.

BEAN CURD

There are four kinds of bean curd—different because of water content: Hard-pressed, good for use in mock meat dishes; Regular, softer but used for deep-frying and for a variety of other uses; Soft, used only for soup, cannot be cut; and real original curd which has had none of the water pressed out. In all of the recipes which follow I use only the "regular" type.

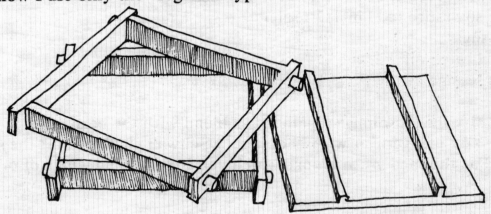

BEAN CURD-COLD-MIXED

This dish is one of the oldest recipes for bean curd and while it is plain, it is very good for hot summer days.

You should use it only as a side dish so don't prepare too much.

2 c bean curd cut in 1/4 x 1/4 inch pieces
2 T soy sauce (add in 1/2 t salt)
1 t sugar
1 T heated oil
1 T sesame oil

Mix the seasonings together and blend with the bean curd.

You can garnish with chopped Sze-chwan pickles (omit the salt in the seasoning) or chopped green onions which you have burned with hot oil.

BEAN CURD & EGGS — CHINESE-FRIED

Heat 2 T of oil very hot. Brown 2 c of diced bean curd, add 1 t salt, and blend well; 20 seconds later pour 3 eggs beaten with 1 t salt on the browning bean curds. Let it set for several seconds than add 1 T of oil through the edges of the whole batch. Turn the batch over. Serve when the eggs are set.

You may need one more T of oil before serving, and chopped green onions are optional—to be beaten with the eggs or added when the eggs are half set. This is a simple but good dish.

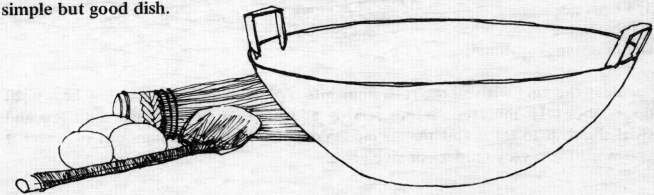

BEAN CURD & EGGS — STEAMED

1 c bean curd, mashed
2 eggs
2 eggs' amount water
  (use broken shell to measure, simple?)
1 T oil
1 t salt
1/4 t pepper
1 t soy sauce
Green onions (optional)

Beat the eggs with all the rest, pour into a pie dish and steam at low heat until done, about 15 minutes. Before serving add another t of soy sauce on top and swirl the dish to let it tint the surface. You can increase the amount of water if you want them very tender—or vice versa.

BEAN CURD—DEEP-FRIED

Cut the curd into 1/2 inch cubes and soak them with 1 c of water and 1 T of salt. Drain and deep-fry at 330° until golden brown all over. This is only the basic procedure for many variations.

BEAN CURD -- STUFFED

Raw bean curd will not be very good for vegetarian cooking, so let us try to use the Deep-fried one.

Cut one of the cube's 6 faces as a slit opening for the stuffing. For stuffing we have very little choice, but enough. Try pre-soaked mushrooms finely chopped; pre-soaked mung-bean-threads, roughly chopped; fewer pre-cooked carrots, finely chopped; mashed fresh bean curd, enough to provide some body; and as many chopped bamboo shoots as carrots.

Season them with soy sauce, sugar, a good amount of oil and some sesame oil. Add some cornstarch to make the mixture sticky. Fill each deep-fried bean curd.

There are several ways to serve this dish: You can poach in seasoned broth for 10 minutes and serve; you can stew them in a pan with water to cover, simmering until the sauce is low, adjusting the taste of the sauce, then thickening and serving; or double frying (this way requires extra care not to over-stuff)—deep fry again for less than a minute.

BEAN — RED

"Red-Bean-Sand" is frequently used as Sweet-stuffing. Soak 2 cups—or more—of red beans overnight. Simmer with water, an inch over the beans, till tender. A wok is a better tool because its edgeless bottom makes it easy to turn the beans during simmering. When the beans are "sand" or pureed, add an equal amount of sugar—2 cups or more—and cook over medium low heat, turning the batch over once in awhile, but never pause too long or it will burn. If beans were well-simmered they will soon become the texture of mashed potatoes.

After about 10 minutes start to add oil. You will need about a cup in all, but add in only small quantities through the cooking procedure. Add the oil always at the edge of the wok to prevent burning or sticking. The color of the whole batch will darken and end a dark shining reddish brown.

This will keep if no moisture gets in. Freeze it in small packages as you probably can not use too much at a time. Use it as a ready-made seasoned stuffing. For bananas you can roll it into a cigarette shape. Oh! Why should I say cigarettes! Shape it into a pencil shape for easy filling of the hollow parts of the banana. For steamed buns, etc., roll it into marble-size or larger balls according to the size of the wrapping.

BEANS – LIMA

LIMA BEANS WITH BRINED VEGETABLES: The particular vegetables I mention here can be found in San Francisco under a Chinese name which bears a work of Red, but the beans are actually completely green.

This could possibly be for the rhythm of the name, and red is a welcome color in China -- who knows if for this reason it determines the fate of China. Coincidentally, Nationalist China's flag was named as the shining sun on the blue sky, upon the Red earth!

If you can't find fresh lima beans in a Chinese market you can still find them in cans.

Simmer 2 cups of lima beans until tender. Drain, but keep the juice. Heat a wok, add 1/4 cup of oil and then 1/2 cup of brined vegetables, lightly squeezed dry; cook for 30 seconds and then add the cooked beans and the juice. Adjust the seasoning. If it is not too salty, use soy sauce instead of salt. If it is too salty use sugar to counteract. If the saltiness is right you still need sugar, but very little, to harmonize the taste—this is one of the cooking tricks—you need at least 2 t of sugar.

BEANS --FRIED LIMA

Soak the beans in water overnight. Drain, but use the water for soup. The beans can be deep-fried over rather low heat till apparently the mositure is almost out. Speaking correctly, this is deep-oil cooking. Strain out the oil, and sprinkle with salt. Use as a side dish for Congee, or eat them as toasted peanuts.

BROCCOLI

There are several varieties. The one I favor has a longer stem and smaller flower heads than the common one. It has a stronger taste of vegetable and usually bears yellowish flowers among the green.

Trim to get rid of the too tough parts. The stem can be peeled and a sizable part saved for other use in cooking. Splitting the flower head should be done from the end of stem or you will break the flowers, the same as in cauliflowers. Tender leaves are used, while the tough ones can be used in another method.

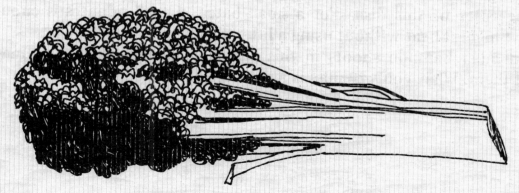

BROCCOLI WITH BAMBOO SHOOTS

This might be the best combination as far as Chinese cooking is concerned as we don't use creamed sauce for this vegetable, while non-Chinese cooking could adapt many different ways to serve.

The bamboo shoots should be cut into slices, and broccoli into thin pieces. Seasoning is limited to salt, a pinch of sugar, and a little wine before serving. During the cooking it is just a simple Chinese-frying. Use water little by little to have enough steam to cook the vegetable. Never try to add in soy sauce, you will spoil the color of this dish. For a small batch, 5 to 7 minutes is enough. Cook always at highest heat without using a lid.

Remember bamboo shoots in this dish are a complement. You may cook it without them. What you will miss is a contrasting color.

GREEN AND WHITE BROCCOLI

To gain the appearance of a dish without bamboo shoots you can parboil cauliflower, drain, and cook with broccoli. Same seasonings as above.

BRUSSEL SPROUTS

2 c Brussel sprouts
4 T oil
2 T soy sauce

1 t salt
2 t sugar

Heat oil, add in the Brussel sprouts. Cover with water, add the seasonings and simmer until tender. Lightly thicken with cornstarch before serving.

For variety, stew the sprouts with bamboo shoots cut into cubes to match or use black mushrooms for a different flavor.

CARROTS

These are used mostly as complements for their color in a Chinese-fried dish.

In conventional cooking of stewed lamb, carrots play a good role to enhance the flavor in addition to adding color. I use them as a back-stage hero in a soy-bean-paste dish, because of their natural sweetness, ease of mashing as puree, and their reddish color.

The problem I faced many times is now solved: Too little soy-bean-paste gives a dish less richness; too much soy-bean-paste turns a dish too salty; blended with cooked cornstarch sauce, it will lose its color, and also the body is too lean.

Puree of carrots answers all those problems. This is absolutely disobeying the classic Chinese recipes for soy-bean-paste. It is cheating—but cheating is not always bad!

The proportion may be: 1 part bean-paste to 1 part mashed carrots. When other complements are to be used, dark soy sauce may be added to reach the right saltiness and color.

CAULIFLOWER

This goes well with a sauce which bears a foreign name and is still a very popular gourmet dish, "Baked Vegetables-in-season." (Only high class restaurants will serve these dishes). I have hundreds of Portuguese friends yet none of them has heard of such a dish in his country. Though it bears a non-Chinese name, I presume that it was invented in China—the cooking method is clearly the Chinese way so I include it here.

"Baked Vegetable-in-season with Portuguese Sauce" gives you the flexibility to choose available vegetables. However, the most frequently used vegetables are cauliflower, carrots, broccoli, and asparagus.

You can use one, two, three, or four different vegetables. Two can be arranged half-and-half or in four parts alternated. Three can be arranged in rows and four kinds in quarters. Never let the white asparagus be next to the cauliflower—they have no contrast in color.

Into a 10-inch oven-proof pie dish put the drained (keep the juice) asparagus from a 15 oz. can. Try to let them occupy a quarter of the whole area. Then in another pan parboil equal amounts of carrots, cauliflower and broccoli. Since these take different times to parboil, start with the carrots; when they have cooked for 5 minutes add the cauliflower, 2 minutes later add the broccoli, and cook another 2 minutes. Drain them all at one time and keep the water for soup or other use. Place the parboiled vegetables in the remaining 3/4 of the pie plate, each in its own quarter.

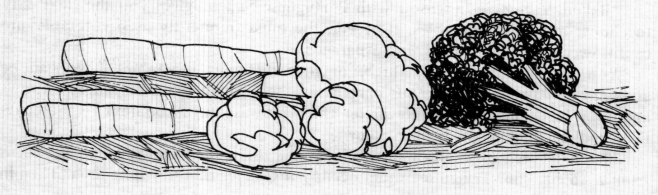

PORTUGUESE SAUCE. You will need sauce enough to fill the dish half full without the vegetables. You can measure the broth you'll need by pouring it into the pie plate to the half way point before you put the vegetables in it. Keep one cup of it asside for mixing the flour and cornstarch.

Using a saucepan, combine 1 t of curry powder with 3 to 6 T of oil. When curry is bubbling add in the pre-measured broth and bring to a boil. Season with salt, approximately 1 t per cup, and add a pinch of sugar. Thicken with the cup of broth which you kept aside to which you have added 2 T of flour and 3 T of cornstarch. Stir well before adding, pouring in slowly and stirring constantly. The sauce should be rather thick for no matter how well you drain the vegetables there is still a lot of moisture in them. Pour the thickened sauce on the vegetables, cover evenly. 20 minutes before serving, heat the oven to 400°, bake for 10 minutes or till the sauce is bubbling. Use the last 2 minutes to brown under the broiler. Serve with plain rice.

CAULIFLOWER WITH SEASONED SOY SAUCE

2 c cauliflower
2 T oil
2 T soy sauce
1 t salt
1 T sugar

Start with hot oil, add in the cauliflower and cook at medium heat for 10-15 seconds. Add the seasoning and enough water to cover. Cook, not simmer, covered, until the water is reduced to very little. You need to check at least once after five minutes to adjust the water if it is too little. Just before serving adjust the seasoning, thicken with 1 t of cornstarch, and garnish with sesame oil.

CHIVES

If you grow your own chives I hope you can find the Chinese variety with flat leaves and sharper taste. Or try the following method to raise yellow chives, which are rated as a delicacy in Chinese cooking due to the effort consumed in cultivation and its delicacy in taste.

The method is based on the sunlight which produces the chlorophyll of greens. Chinese do this only with chives because of their tiny size. The method is very simple. During the day, early in the morning, cover the growing chives with a flower pot (seal the drainage hole). You must not use a tin can which will conduct too much heat and kill the chives. When the sun has set, take away the pot to let them breathe. The result is yellow chives—milder and crunchier.

CHIVES WITH EGGS

This is a very common dish. The amount of chives is optional. Cut into 1 inch lengths. Use eggs as desired, season with salt, beat. Cook chives with 2 T of oil for 30 seconds. Bring the chives to the beaten eggs, start again with hot skillet, add a little oil and cook the mixed batch until firm.

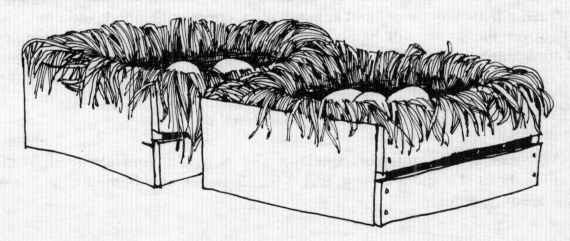

CHIVES WITH BEAN CURD

Chives have a stronger aroma than green onions and can cook longer without losing their flavor.

If you have bean curd on hand, try the following: Cut the curd into domino size and brown on both sides in oil. Add chives cut in the same lengths, season with salt, a little soy sauce, and sugar. Barely cover with water and cook over high heat. Soon the water will be absorbed by the curds. Give them a complete turn and cook until there is no more liquid left. Serve.

COLD MIXED VEGETABLES WITH AGAR-AGAR

Agar-agar is like unflavored gelatin and is made from seaweed. It comes in bundles about 18 inches long and 1 or 2 inches in diameter, and looks like transparent noodles.

2 inch cutting from a bundle of agar-agar
1 medium carrot, peeled, cut in 2" strips
2 c Chinese cabbage, cut same length but wider than carrot
1 c cucumber, peeled, seeded, cut same size as cabbage

Fill a big mixing bowl with water no hotter than 70°, put in the agar-agar. In only a minute or so it will turn soft and become swollen. Pour off the water and squeeze the agar-agar nearly dry. Crisp the carrot in ice water for 15 minutes. Fifteen minutes before serving, sprinkle the cabbage and cucumber lightly with salt and toss gently. Let them rest for 10 minutes and then lightly press out the excess moisture. Add the carrots and the agar-agar, season with Cold-mixing sauce, oil and sesame oil. If you have fresh coriander, chop and add it, too. Don't use parsley.

CONGEE

Once when I was dining with several friends one of us mentioned that a bowlful of congee in the morning, which is a Chinese traditional classic meal, should be considered as Chinese culture.

The basis for congee is rice and water. Proportions vary in different regions of China but you can establish your own preference. It is such a simple matter, the less rice you use the lighter the congee will be, and vice versa. The longer the simmering the smoother it will be.

In certain regions we use left-over rice, add some water and cook 5 minutes. Proper congee should simmer till the water turns thick and milky.

I learned one interesting cooking method from my boyhood school-mate. We were not allowed to cook in our quarters and boiling water was available only during meal time. Some ingenious boy invented this method. You fill a large mouth thermos bottle with rice—about 2 T per serving—and then fill with boiling water (mine takes 2 cups) and cover it at once. Do it at dinner time and by the next morning, if your bottle is a good one, it should still be hot to the touch. The rice will have swelled and become tender.

In northern and eastern China, congee is most often prepared without any seasoning. Certain kinds of dishes are served with congee. Most are salty—often cold, dry, pickled or preserved vegetables. Deep-fried peanuts without shells are a favorite, also lima beans.

In real practice, since Chinese are trained to be economical in youth, we

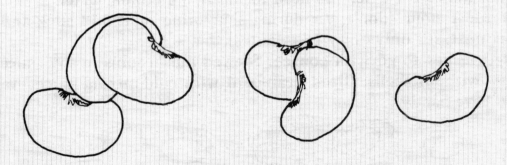

always use leftover dishes from the night before. Leftovers do not have to be re-heated. Purpose is partly to finish the leftover and partly to have something to go with the plain seasonless congee.

For vegetarian seasoned congee you can add peanuts during the simmering, which add taste and smoothness. You can use mushrooms with a light color soy sauce to add more flavor.

Measuring guide: 1/4 c rice (no need to wash), 5 c boiling water.

Simmer for 1 hour (don't stir during simmering or it will stick and maybe burn. If you must, stir only every 15 minutes).

Suggested dishes to go with congee: Stewed mushrooms in soy sauce; Deep-fried peanuts without shells; Diced bean-curd with cold-mixing sauce; Any other leftover you have handy.

CONGEE WITH GINKGO NUTS AND BEAN SKIM

My favorite combination in a plain congee uses two items which are very common in Chinese groceries—Ginkgo Nuts and Bean Skim.

The Ginkgo is a typical huge Chinese tree which bears nuts. Canned Ginkgo is available. Only a little bean skim is needed as its function is to provide smoothness and add the aroma of the soy bean.

For each serving:

2 c water
2 T rice
5 Ginkgo nuts
1 piece of bean skim, about 1" x 5"
  (it comes in sheet form, breakable
  with fingers)

Simmer all together till the nuts are very tender, almost melting.

112

CORIANDER

If you can not distinguish coriander from parsley I hope you say, "I am not a gardener!" Then you cause me to tell that I am not a fisherman because I only recently learned how to distinguish sand dabs from rex sole. Both of the two pairs are quite similar but very much different in taste.

Your chance to find fresh coriander is very slight if you do not live in the vicinity of a Chinese population. For this reason, maybe, coriander is referred to as Chinese parsley.

Its origin was in southern Europe and the Portuguese brought it to China. Its name in Chinese bears clearly a word which hints of westerners.

It is a shade lighter in color than parsley, with flat sawtoothed leaves. It should not be cooked but is used mostly for garnishing. When you chop it include the stem which is crunchy.

CORIANDER PUFFY EGGS — this is **a very Chinese touch**

2 eggs (for one serving)
2 stalks of coriander, 1/4 inch cut
1 t salt
1/8 t pepper powder, optional
1 T oil

   Beat all together. Heat a skillet very hot, add in 2 T of oil, pour in the mixture and let cook for 5 seconds; fold into a roll and cook another 5 seconds. Pour in 1 cup of hot broth, boil for 5 seconds, and serve.

CUCUMBER

When buying cucumbers don't buy the larger ones—in most cases they are overmatured, coarse, and empty. A very good variety is the English Cucumber, a foot long, light pale green, and almost seedless, but not always obtainable.

Trimming—if you like to peel them do so very gently with a peeler. And don't worry if the shape does not allow you to peel completely. If it is young and firm you can leave the seeds or you can cut them lengthwise and scoop out the seeds with a small, thin spoon.

Cutting for slices: try the butterfly-cutting, i.e. first cut 3/4 through, then the second all the way through. It tastes and cooks better. Domino-cutting: for stewing you need big pieces and you can cut in any form you like, but don't you agree that in geometry there is a golden cut? No matter who designs a national flag he follows, somehow, the same rectangular form. It is the same in cooking. We like to have the food cut into a form to please. So follow the domino shape.

CUCUMBER-COLD-MIXED—1 lb of cucumber, peeled and cut into slices or strips with 1/4 cup of cold-mixing sauce (page 49) added five minutes before serving.

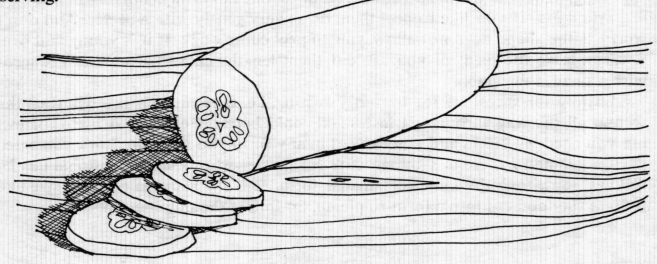

CUCUMBER — QUICK-STEWED

1 lb of cucumber, domino cut
2 T oil
1 t salt
2 T soy sauce
1 t sugar

Heat the oil, add the cucumber, and cook for 15 seconds. Add the seasonings and barely cover with water. Cover with a lid, cook 5 to 10 minutes until the sauce is reduced. Thicken slightly with cornstarch and add sesame oil before serving.

EGGS

   EGG PURSE is actually the westerners' fried egg, but instead of cooking it in its natural round shape we fold one half over the other to form a stuffy round shape which looks like a lady's purse. In a wok this is easy but you can do it by tilting the skillet and folding the egg with a spatula to form the purse. Do this before the egg is set and cook with medium heat. If you like the yolk soft serve with a little more soy sauce; if you want it hard, add 2 T of water and 1 t of soy sauce, and cook until the water is gone.

STEWED EGGS

I've used this dish several times when unexpected visitors arrived just before dinner and I had nothing but eggs and some vegetables. To serve six:

6 eggs
12 dried mushrooms, soaked in hot water
2 c cabbage, sliced
Mung-bean threads, cut in 2 inch lengths
Salt
Soy sauce
Sugar

Fry the eggs and shape into purses as in preceding recipe. While the eggs are cooking and the mushrooms are soaking, cook the cabbage slices in a pot with oil and add the Mung-bean threads. By the time the eggs are done, the cabbage will be half cooked.

Remove the eggs from the pan and set them aside. Put the mushrooms (squeezed dry) into the hot wok or skillet and turn the heat high, add one more T of oil, and let them sizzle for 15 seconds. Pour the cabbage and threads on the mushrooms and arrange the eggs on top.

Fill the wok with water to cover, add salt, soy sauce, and sugar. Cover with a lid and cook until the sauce is reduced and the whole batch is done. Adjust seasoning just before serving, thicken slightly, and don't forget the sesame oil.

MING PORCELAIN EGGS

Ming Porcelain Eggs are actually called Tea Eggs in China but I call them this because of their appearance.

First boil some eggs, starting with cold water over medium heat. Ten minutes after they start to boil, cool them in cold water. Make a broth by boiling 1 tea bag (use red or black but not green) in water for 5 minutes and then add more water to cover the number of eggs you have boiled. Measure the amount of broth now, and for each cup add 1 T of soy sauce, 1 t of salt, 1 whole star aniseed, if you can find it. If you can't, substitute 1 inch of cinnamon stick or some in powder form. Now crack the hard–boiled eggs gently all over with the bottom of a spoon. Immerse the eggs in the broth, bring to a boil and simmer for 30 minutes. Let stand overnight.

Serve as a cold dish. Peel them, cut into wedges, and serve with soy sauce and sesame oil added. I guarantee that they will look like Ming Porcelain, or your smile back!

TIGER EGGS

Tiger Eggs are a famous dish in central China. I was taught to deep-fry peeled hard-boiled eggs to achieve wrinkled skins. After stewing in soy sauce, eggs bear a design which they likened to the look of tiger's hide.

But I no longer deep-fry them. It spills too much. No, I cook them in oil. Start with cold oil and the shelled eggs, at medium heat. When the temperature exceeds the boiling point the moisture in the eggs will begin to bubble. Then you should turn the heat lower and continue to cook until the eggs are well fried. Remove the eggs from the pan and dump immediately into cold water. Put them back into the pan, fill with water and seasonings of your choice, simmer until the seasoning gets into the egg white. The longer you simmer the saltier the eggs will be. Serve anyway you like, whole or in halves, hot or cold.

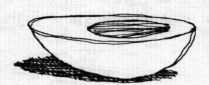

EGGPLANT -- QUICK STEWED

Cut the eggplant with the roll-cut. Heat the oil and put in the eggplant. A little more oil than usual is used as this vegetable absorbs a lot of oil. Turn the pieces over and over for ten seconds. Add in soy sauce, sugar, and only enough water to produce steam for cooking. Cover with a lid and cook at high heat for three minutes. Check the moisture. By now you may need to add in a little more water. Cover again. Check again and if necessary, add water, and cover. When eggplant has cooked about ten minutes it should be done. If you like the eggplant firmer, you may shorten the cooking time. When the dish is done there should be no excess sauce and the eggplant should be soft but not soggy. Serve it with a small amount of sesame oil as garnish.

For a different but pleasant taste you may add a quarter-size piece of finely chopped ginger root, 1 mashed clove of garlic, and 1 teaspoon of vinegar to the principal seasoning of soy sauce, sugar, and sesame oil. These ingredients are mostly used for mocking sea-food dishes.

EGGPLANT – STEAMED

If the eggplants are rather long and thin cut them in half lengthwise. If they are large and round, cut them crosswise in pieces no more than an inch thick. Put them in a dish. Line them with spaces between as forming a grill. Then add the second layer at right angles to form a mesh. The spaces left in between will help them cook fast and evenly. Prepare some fresh crushed garlic and salt or use ready-made garlic salt. Sprinkle each slice with garlic salt on one side only. Now add in some soy sauce, vinegar, and a pinch of sugar. Cook about ten minutes. You may check as often as you like. Take out the cooked eggplant halves or slices. Cool them a little so you can handle them. Mix them with a little sesame oil. This dish may be served warm or cold as a salad. Most Chinese prefer it warm.

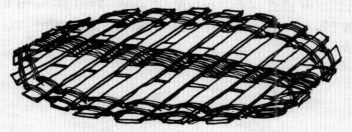

FLOWERS IN CHINESE VEGETARIAN COOKING

The Chinese use several different flowers; dried wild yellow lily, roses, or cinnamon blossoms.

Rose petals are used to make syrup. Dry them thoroughly in sunshine, chop them fine or pulverize in your blender. Add the roses to a simple syrup you make with equal parts of sugar and water when the syrup reaches 215°. Stir well and store in a jar. Use this as you would honey—on bread or hot cakes, or as a dressing for rice pudding.

You can also make your own rose jam. Wash the fresh-picked rose petals and drain off excess moisture. Put them in a bowl covered, but not buried, with sugar and leave them for several days. Blend the soggy petals in your blender and add more sugar to reach the consistency of jam. You should keep this refrigerated.

Cinnamon blossoms can be prepared in the same manner as the rose jam but use less sugar.

LUFFA

This plant is best known for its use as a towel gourd but in China one variety when picked very young is an elegant vegetable.

The sharp edges should be peeled off and the green part cut into thick slices or rolling cut. If too thin it will become soggy in cooking.

Luffa soup has a spongy texture and a very nice fragrance. Boil Mung-bean-threads in water, with seasonings to taste, until soft. Add cut luffa at the last minute and serve.

LUFFA AND ONIONS This is an established Chinese combination.

1 c luffa in thick slices
1 c onions, in wedges to match
1 T oil

   Heat the oil, cook the onions first; after 1 minute add the luffa, season with salt, soy sauce, a pinch of sugar and very little water. Cook for another minute and serve.

LOTUS

Because the lotus grows in a muddy pond which symbolizes the dirty (sinful) society and yet has pure white and clean flowers the Chinese describe an outstanding young person in a rotten generation as "The Lotus in the Pond."

The lotus plant is completely useful to the Chinese. The crunchy roots are very tasty eaten as fresh fruit—chilled, peeled and sliced. The roots can be dried and ground into a powder which, when added to boiling water and stirred swiftly, is used as a hot sweet snack with sugar.

Lotus leaves are often used instead of grape leaves for wrapping of other foods to which they impart a pleasant fragrance.

For lotus root soup just peel the roots, cut into thick slices or chunks. Simmer in water with salt for an hour or until the lotus turns flakey. A very nice soup.

LOTUS ROOT STUFFED WITH RICE is typically Chinese. Soak rice in water with salt and soy sauce; cut the end of the lotus and fill the holes in the cut section with the rice. You don't have to stuff the roots very tightly as the rice will swell and fill the holes neatly after steaming for an hour or more. Cut into 1/2 inch slices and serve.

For Chinese-frying the lotus root should be cut into thin strips. Heat the oil and simply add the lotus strips. You can season them with salt or a little soy sauce or with sugar and vinegar, which is Sweet and Sour but very much milder than the taste of Sweet and Sour Pork. With both ways of seasoning the lotus will be done when the sauce begins to turn sticky and gray in color.

131

MUSTARD GREENS

The tips of the leaves of mustard greens make a soup with a light, bitter, refreshing taste. You need nothing but some soy sauce, oil, and water too, of course.

The thicker parts of the greens are more suitable for Chinese frying. Strong wine should be added during the cooking, 1 t of dry cooking wine is enough. It is done before it turns soggy and dull in color. Soy sauce adds taste but it hurts the color—try to add it just before serving as a garnish.

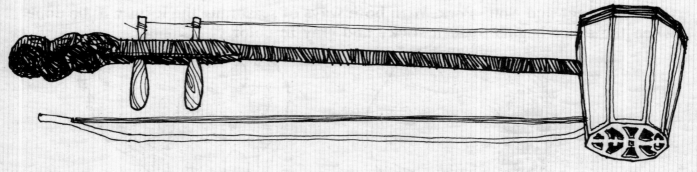

PEARS

This is very Chinese. Wash firm fruit and cut off the top 1/5. Hollow out the bottom 4/5—actually you are just removing the hard core and seeds. Fill the cavity with rock sugar, replace the top and hold together with several tooth picks. Steam the pears for an hour at low heat and serve warm as dessert.

Like honey your grandmother used to give you for soothing your throat, my grandmother gave this to us. It has no medicinal value but it does have a lot of touching love which can never be forgotten.

133

PEPPERS

Peppers are used frequently in Chinese cooking for their color and their crunchiness if not overcooked. Since they also give the oil a nice aroma, many dishes start with peppers to season the oil and proceed with the rest.

When we use them for stuffing we cut them into small wedges—their natural cavity is just right for filling, which in the Chinese way should be no thicker than 1/4 inch.

PEPPERS, OIL-COOKED

This is the only dish in which Chinese use peppers without other complements. For this, use the smaller variety and cook them whole. Wash and dry them first, then cook in oil at low heat (300°) until the skins are wrinkled and they are soft. Drain, garnish with soy sauce, sugar, and some vinegar, if you like. Stuff them in a large-mouth jar and let it stand overnight. Turn the jar upside down several times during the cooling. Serve as a pleasant cold-dish complement.

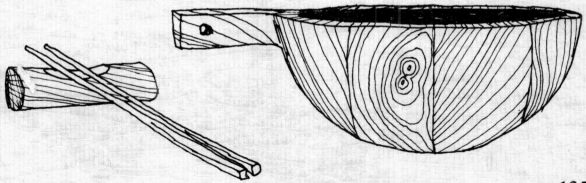

PEPPERS AND BAMBOO SHOOTS

1 c pepper strips
1 c bamboo shoots strips
1 T soy sauce
1/2 t salt
1/4 t sugar

Cook the peppers with 2 T of oil until tender, about 5 minutes. You'll need a little water, too. Add the bamboo shoots, then the seasoning, and cook until the sauce disappears. Serve.

PEPPERS AND BEAN CURD

1 c bean curd strips, pre-fried
1 c pepper strips
2 T soy sauce
1/2 t sugar

Cook the peppers in oil first; when almost done add the pre-fried bean curd, the seasoning and a little water. When the sauce is gone, garnish with sesame oil, and serve.

PEPPERS—STUFFED

Sweet bell peppers are best for this. Cut them into wedges about bite size.

Stuffing:

1 c mashed potatoes

1/2 c bean curd, prefried, chopped to pea size
  (fry in slices, then chop)

3—4 dry mushrooms, presoaked, squeezed
  dry and cut to pea size

1 egg

1 t salt

1 t soy sauce

1 t sugar

1 t oil

Blend all together. Fill the pepper wedges and use a little oil to brown the stuffed peppers on the bottom side—low heat for about 1 minute is enough. There should be only one layer in your skillet. Add water to a depth of 1/4 inch and simmer at high heat until the peppers are soft and done. Remove them to a serving platter, thicken the remaining sauce with some cornstarch and pour evenly on top of each of the stuffed peppers.

SQUASH

In a Chinese cookbook I don't like to include items which are not established in Chinese kitchens. There are only a few kinds of squash which we use regularly but there is no reason that you cannot try other kinds using the cooking method according to texture.

Fuzzy Squash must have a proper name but I do not know it. I do know it to be fuzzy all over with both ends round and to be apple green. The fuzz should be removed carefully by scraping—don't overdo because the green part is very tasteful. Cut the squash in slices and again in strips.

1 c fuzzy squash in 5 inch strips
1-1/2 t salt
2 T oil

Just heat the oil, add the squash and salt, a little water, and cook until soft. It will cook quickly and since the squash is naturally sweet you need no sugar.

SQUASH WITH MUNG-BEAN THREADS

1 c fuzzy squash in 5 inch strips
1 oz dried mung-bean threads, soaked and cut
 in 2 inch lengths
2 t salt
4 T oil

   If the threads are well soaked; they and the squash will take the same cooking time. If not, you should pre-cook them for several minutes. Add the threads when the squash has been in the oil for several seconds. Add just enough water for the threads to absorb.

141

PUMPKIN

You make pumpkin pie in America but we make pumpkin soup in China. Actually, this is more of a one-dish meal since it has in it a fair amount of dough.

1 lb of pumpkin cut into domino size
2 qts of broth or water

Make a dough or batter of 3/4 cups of water to 1 cup of flour in a small bowl. Remove the cooked pumpkin from the broth. Pour the batter slowly (about a tablespoon at a time) into the broth, keeping the pourings separate if you can. Keep the broth barely boiling until you have finished adding the batter, then increase the heat somewhat and cook for several minutes until the dough is done. By now the soup is cloudy and thick. Return the pumpkin and add a little oil for smoothness. Serve.

RADISHES

I think of these as Crunchy Red Radish Balls.

Trim the radishes neatly of leaves and tiny roots and wash in cold water. Using a small thin knife cut slits from one end an eighth of an inch apart. Cut about 3/4ths of the way through the radish but no further. Now turn the radish to its other end and repeat the process.

Turn the radish upside down, give it a quarter turn and start cutting slits again. When you reach the center, turn to the other end. You end up with two sets of slits at right angles to each other. The result is delicious and the taste is entirely different from the conventional way of slicing radishes, no matter how thin you make the slices.

Sprinkle salt lightly on the cut radishes and toss them thoroughly. Set them aside in the refrigerator for at least 30 minutes. Bring them out and fold them in paper towels, five or six at a time, and squeeze firmly but not so hard as to break them. Marinate a cup of radishes in a T of soy sauce, 1/2 T of vinegar, 1/2 T of sugar and 1 t of sesame oil.

WON TON DOUGH

To make this is not difficult but it is rather tedious. If you have access to a Chinese grocery you can buy commercially made Won Ton dough but I include detailed instructions on how to make it yourself for those readers without access to the manufactured kind.

You will need:

a good size board, or a wooden table top
a long rolling pin—20 inches cut from a broom stick will do
a cheesecloth bag (4" x 8") to use as a duster
1 lb all-purpose flour
4 medium eggs
1/4 c cornstarch (put into the cloth bag, tied closed)

Put the flour into a mixing bowl, dig a hole in the middle and break the eggs into the hole. You may need to add a very little amount of water or flour to

145

adjust the consistency of the dough. Cover with a lid and let stand for 5 minutes. Remove lid and knead the dough well, making final adjustment of water or flour. Let stand another 5 minutes. Now roll it out into a large sheet as for a pizza.

Dust the sheet lightly with the cornstarch and, starting at one edge, roll the whole sheet onto the broom stick. Don't roll too tightly since you will have to remove the stick, leaving a rolled tube of the dough.

Now, with both hands holding the broom stick, press the rolled dough at right angles, at about half-inch intervals. Start at the middle and work to both ends. If you dusted the dough with cornstarch you should now have no difficulty in unrolling the pressed dough. Unrolled, it will be larger and thinner. Gently roll and smooth all over with the broom stick, dusting frequently. Repeat the whole operation several times and the dough will be thin enough. After the last unrolling cut the dough into 3-inch squares and they are ready for stuffing. You can cut the irregular shapes left over into 1/6-inch strips and you have fresh noodles.

DUMPLINGS

To make dumplings is also very easy but there is one very important thing to remember—It is Boiling water against Cold Water!

Dumpling to be cooked by boiling should be made with COLD water.

Dumpling to be cooked by steaming should be made with BOILING water.

Dumpling to be cooked by pan-frying should be made with COLD water.

To make the dough, put the all-purpose flour into a mixing bowl to which you will add water, nothing else. Boiling or Cold? Make that decision first. Ratio of flour to water will be about 2 to 1. The rest is the same as with Won Ton dough—let stand, knead, let stand.

Shape the dough into a roll about a foot long and an inch in diameter; cut into slices about 1/4-inch thick using a flour-dusted knife. Dust the pieces with flour and flatten them as a cookie with the heel of your hand.

Now you need a piece of broom stick about 7 inches long. Hold the cookie shaped dough with your thumb in the middle of the top and three fingers underneath. Let only the near side touch the table. With your other open hand roll the broom stick back and forth on the hand held dough several times. Rotate the dough and roll the stick back and forth again. With 5 to 7 rollings and turns the dough will be thin enough. The middle will be somewhat thicker than the edges, which is why you held on to the dough with one hand.

You are now ready to fill with any stuffing you like.

To seal, the easiest way is to fold the dough into a half-moon and pinch the edges tightly with your fingers, but it does not look pretty. A simple improvement is to pinch two tucks on one side of the half-moon. With these tucks the sealed dumpling will curl to one side somehow.

It is especially necessary if you decide to pan-fry them, as it will sit nicely and eventually will bear a golden brown crust, which is the famous Quo Tik (pan-stickers).

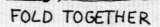

FOLD TOGETHER

TUCKS

148

TO COOK WON TON OR DUMPLINGS

Boiling is simple. Put the won ton or dumplings into a big pot of boiling water. When it boils again add one ladle of cold water which breaks the boiling. Cook until it boils once more, strain and serve.

If you don't have a steamer it is easy to improvise. In a large deep pot have water about 1/2 inch deep; rest a small bowl on the bottom, the top of which is higher than the level of the water. On this you will put the dish holding the food

to be steamed. This dish should be covered with a paper towel dampened with water and a little oil and squeezed dry. The dumplings rest on top of the paper. Put the dish of dumplings or won ton in only after the water is boiling, cover, and let them steam for five minutes. Steamed dumplings made with boiling-water-dough will have shiny surfaces. To eat them, dip in soy sauce garnished with a little sesame oil.

An automatic electric skillet is an excellent tool to pan-fry won ton or dumplings. Turn the control to 350°, put in 2 T of oil and let it run all over the cooking surface. When the temperature gets to 250° you can begin to put in the dumplings. To help give a better crust add half a cup of water mixed with 1 t vinegar. Cover and let it go. When the light blinks off, the 350° has been reached. Lift the lid and drop the condensation back into the pan, cover again and when the light blinks off again it is time to serve them bottoms up to preserve the crispiness. You may have to try this several times to be sure of your skillet's heat control to give you golden brown Quo Tik.

STUFFINGS

Stuffing preparation varies with the manner of cooking whatever you are stuffing—won ton, dumplings, or egg rolls.

STUFFING TO BE BOILED

1/2 c soaked mung-bean threads, cut in tiny pieces
1/4 c soaked mushrooms, cut tiny
1/4 c bean curd (harder type), mashed
  (if you don't have bean curd,
  substitute 2 scrambled eggs)

1 t salt
1 T light soy sauce
1/2 t sugar
1/4 t pepper powder, optional
1 T cooking oil

Mix all together, stuff into won ton or dumplings, boil them and serve.

STUFFING FOR BUNS OR DUMPLINGS TO BE STEAMED

1 c green vegetables (Chinese cabbage, spinach,
  mustard greens) salted and squeezed, chopped.
1 c scrambled eggs
1/2 c bamboo shoots, cooked and chopped
1/4 c soaked mushrooms, chopped
2 t salt

2 T soy sauce
1 t sugar
3 T cooking oil
1/2 t pepper powder
1/4 c broth with gelatin

The moisture content of stuffing must vary with the method of final cooking. When you cook by steaming, the buns or dumplings will be drier than when boiled. So with this stuffing you must add the broth with gelatin. Cook the broth with unseasoned gelatin—about half the quantity advised for jelly. Let the mixture cool and fold in the rest of the ingredients. Stuff the dumplings, or buns, or egg rolls and steam.

STUFFING FOR DEEP FRIED WON TON

1/2 c cooked carrot, cut in tiny pieces
1/2 c onion strips, pre-cooked with oil, only half done
1/2 c green pepper, in strips and cooked as the onions
1/2 c celery strips, also cooked as the onions
2 T soy sauce
2 t salt
2 T cooking oil
2 T cornstarch

Mix all together and stuff the won ton. You can also use this stuffing in mashed potato croquettes shaped in ping pong ball size.

2 c mashed potatoes, 2 t salt, 1/2 t pepper.

For variation add two beaten eggs, 1/2 c bread crumbs, and an additional t of salt. Roll the balls in the bread crumbs before deep-frying.

THUNDERING SOUP

This is a very interesting dish which is commonly called "Sizzling Soup" in gourmet Chinese restaurants, but I change the name to "Thundering" which sounds more interesting.

There are two separate parts to this dish which come together just as you serve.

Well ahead you can make rice crust this way: Use a small pot to cook half a cup of unwashed rice with 1-1/2 cups of water. Cook covered over medium heat for 5 minutes. Then put the rice and the water into a small baking tray and spread evenly to cover the entire tray. Spread evenly with a flat bottom spoon, dipping in cold water, so that the layer of rice is no more than 2 grains thick. Now put the tray in a 230° oven for about an hour. Check the dryness and when it is firm and almost dry as a biscuit, remove from the oven and let cool. When cool enough to handle, cut the layer into domino shapes. You can dry them further in the sun and keep them as you do biscuits—don't put them in the refrigerator.

Now for the soup part. To make four servings:

4 c broth, seasoned with 1 t salt and 1 T light soy sauce
8 soaked mushrooms, simmered well already in the broth
12 slices of bamboo shoots
12 sugar peas to be added to the boiling soup 1 minute
  before serving.

While the soup is boiling, deep fry the dominoes of rice crust until they are golden brown, strain them out and put into a warmed bowl. Pour the soup into another larger bowl and carry both to the table. Dump the deep-fried rice crust into the soup and listen to the thunder. You can add several drops of sesame oil at the time you put in the rice crust.

TOMATO

Since the tomato was introduced to the Chinese by westerners its use in Chinese vegetarian cooking is limited. If you have bean curd, try the recipe below. Their textures are nicely matched and it is a colorful combination.

12 dominoes of bean curd
1 tomato, cut in wedges or squares
1 t salt
1 t sugar
2 T oil

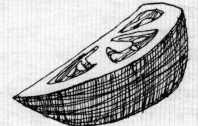

Heat the oil, brown the bean curds lightly on both sides. Add the tomato, the seasoning and a little water. Simmer for 5 minutes. The sauce should be thickened before serving.

/TOMATO AND EGG SOUP

1 tomato, firm and cut into thin wedges
1 egg, beaten
3 c broth or water
1-1/2 t salt
1/8 t sugar
1/2 T oil

When the broth or water boils, add the tomato and the seasoning. Lower the heat a little, slowly pour in the beaten egg, wait and simmer at very low heat for about 15 seconds. Gently stir it with a spoon to avoid the egg sticking to the bottom. When the egg has set, serve.

Do you notice that the amount of sugar is less than in a conventional dish? That is because soup should not contain sugar. But sugar should always follow the vinegar. Tomato is acid so a little amount of sugar is added. Simple touches like this, when rightly done, turn a barely acceptable soup into deliciousness.

TURNIPS -- DRIED

There are many ways to use these in vegetarian cooking and drying your own turnips is part of the fun of Chinese cooking.

Wash the turnips and wipe them dry and then cut into slices first and then into 1/4-inch thick strips. Spread the strips on a paper towel and place in a windy area to dry. usually overnight is enough. If you start the drying during the day, loosen them from the towel and give them a tossing before you go to bed.

When they are dry, spread them out well and sprinkle them evenly with salt. Toss as if you were tossing a green salad to let the salt mix well with the whole batch.

Now you need sunshine and it is not likely that singing "My Only Sunshine" will help you. Pray for your sunshine and if the Lord doesn't listen to you, you better obey Him and give up the rest.

Because of the salt the sun will never completely dry the curing turnips, drier, yes, but never completely. This allows the turnip strips to absorb more sunshine and the rays will change the color, taste, and shape. You don't need strong sunlight. I used to make mine inside on the kitchen counter where the sunshine struck. Toss them each day to help them dry evenly. After several days they will be smaller, dark in color and have a fragrant aroma. Keep them in a bottle for later use.

DRIED TURNIPS WITH VEGETABLES

These can be a very valuable addition to your fresh vegetables. The Chinese have a special nickname for them which translates approximately to "meaty vegetables." You can think of them as mock meat and use them in many ways with many different vegetables.

Dried turnips cook quickly with a little water and sauce added. Think of them as not-quite-dehydrated vegetables—and remember that they are already lightly salted when you are judging seasoning.

TURNIPS WITH GREEN PEPPER

1 part dried turnips and 2 parts green pepper strips, seasoned with soy sauce and sugar, is both tasty and colorful.

TURNIPS WITH BEAN CURD

Quick-stew bean curd with the dried turnips and the curds will pick up the turnip flavor. The oil should be on the rich side.

MOCKED MEAT CHOP SUEY

When you add dried turnips to this common dish you make it twice as good to eat. The turnips should be at least 1/3 the amount of the rest of the vegetables. You serve this over Chinese-fried noodles and call the dish, "Chinese-fried Noodles with Mocked Meat." I like that name better than Chow Mien.

161

TURNIP STRIPS WITH GREEN ONIONS

If you don't like this dish you really convince me that you are against turnips. This is an excellent cold-mixed dish which is especially simple and delightful on a hot summer day.

1 lb turnips, cut in 1/8" x 1/8" x 2" strips
2 stalks of green onions
2 stalks of coriander, if available (don't use parsley)
1/4 c cold-mixing sauce
1/4 c oil

Salt the strips with 1 t of salt sprinkled evenly. Give the turnips a thorough tossing and put them in the refrigerator for 15 minutes, toss again and leave them in the refrigerator for another 15 minutes. Now have the green onions finely chopped and the coriander, too. (No parsley, please! I am so anxious because I am trying my best to convince you that in Chinese vegetarian cooking turnips are delicious.)

After the 30 minutes in the refrigerator, treat the turnips (see Salting and Squeezing, page 38) and place them in a dish as a pyramid. Flatten the top and form a crater as in a volcano, deep enough to hold the chopped green onion and the coriander, if you have it and like it. The coriander should go into the hollow first, then the onions. Now heat the 1/4 cup of oil in the smallest pan you have—heat it until it smokes and then pour on the green onions. Cover the whole surface and if you have any left, pour over the sides of the mounded turnips. Now, add the cold-mixing sauce and toss the whole thing and serve. Be sure that the turnips are chilled. If they are not, return the dish to the refrigerator to regain its coldness.

TURNIP FRITTERS

1 lb turnips, cut in thin strips   1 t pepper powder
1 c all-purpose flour   1 t sugar
3 t salt or to taste   4 stalks green onions, chopped coarsely

Heat a wok, add 2 T of oil, and cook the turnips with salt until they turn soft. Don't overcook—8 minutes should be about right. During the cooking a small amount of water should be added to create steam. Use a lid, of course.

Now cool it down, blend in the flour, pepper, sugar, and green onion. You are making a batter for fritters and you must adjust the water for density.

In another pan have oil ready for deep-frying, keeping the temperature at 300°. Use a soup ladle for the fritters—dip it first into the oil then fill an inch deep with the batter. Gently immerse the filled ladle into the oil, hold it straight for about 30 seconds and by then the batter should be firm enough so that you can easily drop it free in the oil. When golden brown all over remove, drain and cool in a rack. Check the saltiness of the first one and adjust the saltiness of the batter.

TURNIP DOMINO

In China this is a popular snack for which you will need rice flour—you can buy it or make your own this way: Cook the rice as usual (or use leftover— and let it dry completely in the oven or sunshine). When completely dry put the rice in your blender and make it as fine as possible.

1 lb turnips, cut in thin strips
1 c rice flour
2 stalks green onions, chopped fine

2 t salt
1/4 t pepper

Cook the turnips with 3 T of oil and very little water until soft. Blend in all the rest.

Oil a mold such as a pie dish and fill to a depth of about 1/2 inch with the cooked turnips. Steam at medium heat till the mixture is firm, about 30 minutes. Let it cool, unmold, and cut into domino shapes. With a little oil, grill both sides of the dominoes until light brown. Use rather low heat.

WATER CHESTNUTS

When fresh good quality chestnuts are available, you serve as fruit. When steamed with the skins on, the texture is quite different. Both methods are used by street vendors in China and they use a thin bamboo skewer to hold their products. Chinese rarely use canned water chestnuts but they are popular around the world. I have seen many invented recipes by non-Chinese which never fail to include water chestnuts as an authentic Chinese touch. To them porcelain is China and water chestnuts could have been called China-nuts.

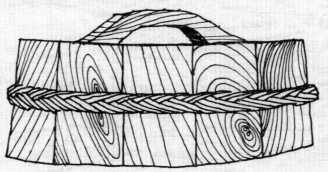

SUGGESTED MENU FOR A 4-COURSE VEGETARIAN DINNER

This is only an example but it is based on reasonable rules for making a menu. Other combinations would be too many to be mentioned but you can make alterations and modifications according to your situation.

Although these are Chinese meals, I put the soup first as nowadays many Chinese do as westerners do.

Soup: Bean Curd & Salted Vegetables
Cold: Assorted Vegetable Strips
Entree: Deep-fried Cauliflower
Maine Course: Stewed Mushrooms

Remember that a cold dish can always be completely prepared and arranged on a serving platter in advance. Soup and stew can be ready ahead of time too, and you need only a minute to put them into a bowl or casserole.

A Chinese-frying dish will take you only a few minutes.

INTRODUCTION TO MOCK DISHES

Chinese Buddist monks have long been famous for their vegetarian cooking and the food they serve is part of the attraction to outsiders who visit their temples. They specialize in mocking all kinds of meat, not only in appearance, but color and texture. A good vegetarian dinner can be very impressive for its creativity and painstaking work in preparation and just as delicious as meat dishes, if not more so.

MOCK SWEET AND SOUR PORK

Probably you know about this famous dish. You should prepare the sauce before cooking the rest of the dish and I give you the recipe in parts—you decide the size of the part.

3 parts sugar
3 parts white vinegar
3 parts ketchup

1 part soy sauce
3 parts water

Bring all ingredients to a boil and boil for two minutes. Thicken to a sauce with a cornstarch mixture.

To mock the pork, use shelled walnut or pecan halves which have been heated in a 220° oven for 15 minutes to insure crispness.

Make a batter of beaten egg, flour, and water to coat crispy nuts for deep-frying. The oil for deep-frying should be at 300°—hotter will burn the nuts. Drop the nuts into the batter and pick out with a small spoon, leaving only enough batter on each nut to cover entirely. The batter will be sticky and running so you have to scrape the bottom of the spoon on the rim of the batter bowl before carrying it to the oil. Turn the nuts over once for even deep-frying. When they are cooked remove them from the oil and keep them in a warmed dish.

After cooking the nuts, pour all but two tablespoons of the cooking oil into its proper container. Now the wok is hot enough for immediate cooking.

While the nuts have been cooking you should have prepared complements—in the same amount as the nuts and cut the same size. Again I give you the recipe in parts.

1 part firm tomato
1 part fresh pineapple or unsweetened canned pineapple
1 part green bell pepper
1 part onion

Turn the heat highest under the wok and Chinese-fry the pepper and onions for 10 seconds; add the sweet and sour sauce and cook for 50 seconds. Now add the tomato and pineapple and cook another 5 seconds. Add the fried nuts, turn off the heat, stir the sauce to cover all the nuts, and serve.

MOCKED FISH WITH SAUCE

Though I sometimes feel that I am a failure because I have committed too many mistakes in my life, I must confess that I was and am still a very lucky man.

I was born into a family in which my grandfather was a never-resting exporter of rawhide and feathers and yet he took all of us touring around famous summer resorts every year. This blessed enjoyment can never be forgotten and I wonder if it will ever repeat in my coming years.

On the eastern coast of China there is a small island called Monte Pu-tu where monks and vacationers dream of paradise. There I experienced too many delicious vegetarian meals to remember them all.

I just could not understand how those monks could mock so many dishes and make them look so real. They would go so far as to arrange neatly bamboo shoots in a comb shape as the bones for a fish! They mocked the skin of the fish with bean-skim, wrapping mashed potatoes in fish shape, and after deep-frying it looked very real.

172

I suggest that you not try to mock the bones with bamboo shoots, but you can do the rest. To mock the body of the fish start with mashed cooked bean curd and also potatoes. Season with salt and pepper, add oil to make it smooth and cornstarch to make it sticky. Now shape a fish to your liking--it should be a

most common shape or you will have to tell people it is a fish! The batch should be rather dry or it will be difficult to shape.

Now, wet some bean skims to soften them, use larger sheets as the bottom wrapping, place the shaped mocked fish on it, and complete the wrapping. You may have to use several pieces to do the whole job.

You can now do something that the monks on Monte Pu-tu could not since they had no ovens. Brush the bean skims with oil and broil slowly till bubbles are plentiful and all over. Don't worry about the bottom side. Set the oven for 250° and in 15 minutes the stuffing should be hot enough.

While the mock fish is heating you can prepare some sauce. Sweet and Sour? Soy-sauce Sauce? Ginger Sauce? How do I know which one you like? My wife has a very simple way to make her choice. If the weather is warm she might like Sweet and Sour. If the weather is cold she might like Ginger Sauce. And normally she would like Soy-sauce Sauce. It sounds simple but the problem is to define her warm and cold, so only she knows what sauce she likes. So will you.

MOCK MEAT BALLS OF TURNIP AND POTATO

In this the turnip mocks the fat part of pork.

1 c mashed potato (drier is better)
1 c turnips, 1/4" slices, 3/4 pre-cooked
1-1/2 t salt
1 t sugar
1/4 t pepper
1 egg
1 t cornstarch

Mix all together and form into balls about 2 inches in diameter. Roll them in flour, firming the flour by pressing gently with both hands. Deep-fry until the crust is desired color. Serve just like a real meat ball, with ketchup or other sauce.

MOCKED PRAWN ON TOAST

4 slices white sandwich bread, trimmed, cut in 4 squares
1/2 lb of potato, boiled with skin, peeled and mashed
1 small carrot, peeled, cooked 3/4 done, chopped fine
1 stalk green onion, chopped
1-1/2 t salt
1/8 t pepper

Mix everything except the bread squares together with 1 T of oil and 1 t of cornstarch. Brush the bread squares with salted (1/4 t) beaten egg. Shape the mixture into a prawn-shaped crescent and place on bread. Press the bread mocked side down into breadcrumbs and fry face down in hot oil for 10 seconds, then turn to other side until bread is golden brown.

Dear Readers:

It is time to say goodbye until, as I hope, I can finish another book— *The Art of Being a Lazy Cook.*

Being intelligently lazy, many persons become famous for their machines, systems, and knowledge to save our effort, time, and money.

I am not intelligent, neither am I wise; but I have observant eyes and have watched others in the kitchen. Many experienced cooks are artfully lazy and yet earn hearty compliments on their cooking. I think that if we can follow some of their art, we can spend less effort, time, and money on our cooking.

I don't mind if you don't like to cook, but don't "hate" to cook, or my sincere invitation to you to share some of my infallible cooking secrets will be useless.

Cook with a lot of LOVE   Just yours,
Serve with a SMILE
      and   Gary Lee
Occasionally, you need some LUCK.   San Francisco, 1972

INDEX

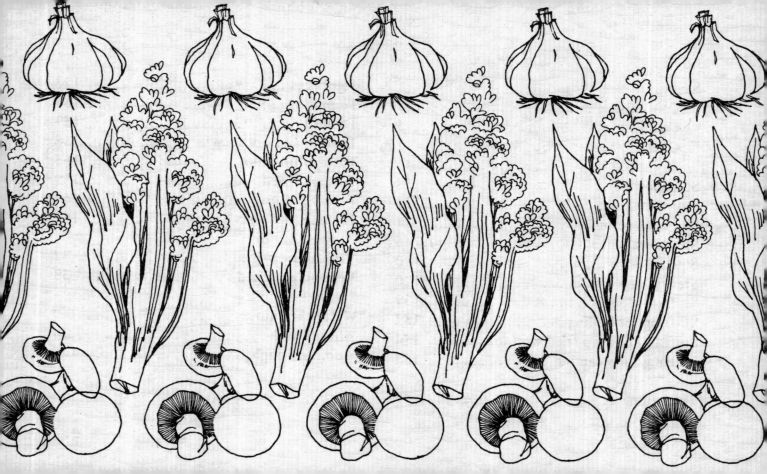